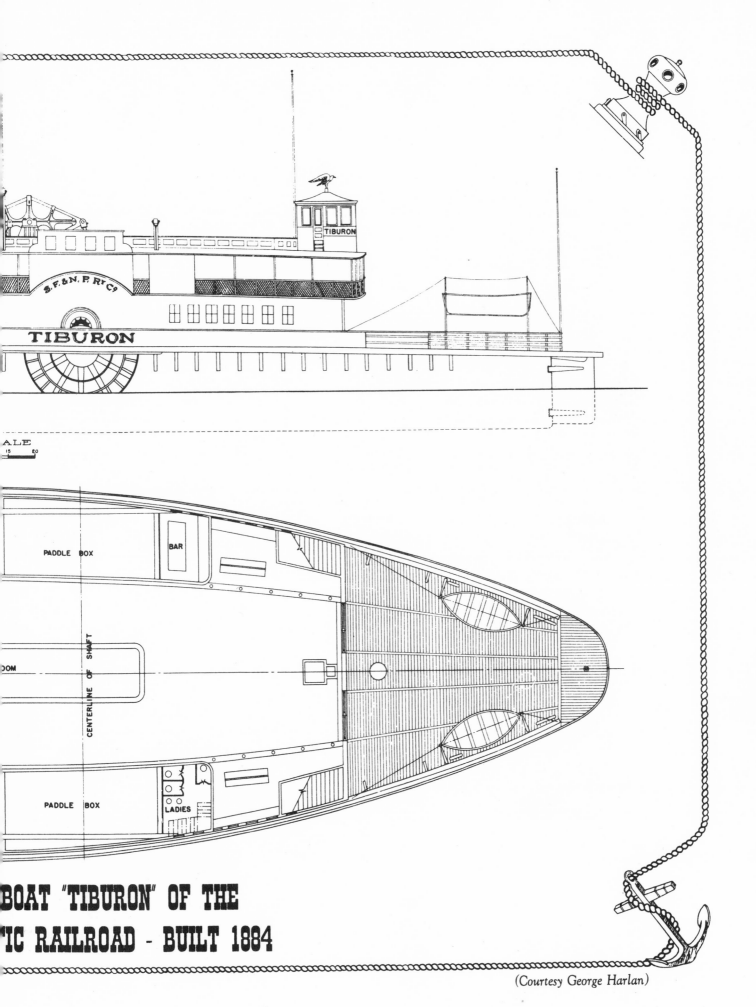

TIBURON

S.F. & N.P. RY Cº

BAR

PADDLE BOX

CENTERLINE OF SHAFT

PADDLE BOX

LADIES

BOAT "TIBURON" OF THE
'IC RAILROAD - BUILT 1884

(Courtesy George Harlan)

To: 'Edmundo' &
Pamela!
fn: 'CHAPER'!
6/86

Pictorial History of
TIBURON

(Philip Molten, Photographer)

SPONSORED BY
THE LANDMARKS SOCIETY OF TIBURON AND BELVEDERE
ON THE OCCASION OF THE TIBURON CENTENNIAL

Pictorial History of
TIBURON
A California Railroad Town

Edited by James Heig

Louise Teather
Historian

Philip Molten
Archivist

SCOTTWALL ASSOCIATES ~ SAN FRANCISCO, CALIFORNIA
1984

Acknowledgments

Many people helped to make this book possible, and we are grateful to all of them: to Adair Lara of Scottwall Associates, for her part in the writing and editing of this book; to Beverly Bastian Meyers, who contributed enormous energy, much information, and several extremely good ideas; to Lawrence Reed Peterson, who selflessly gave of his time and expertise in aiding with the design and layout; to Lawrence Dinneen and the staff of the Bancroft Library for their help in providing pictures; to Joan Krivda, secretary of the Landmarks Society, for her unstinting labors; to Keith Morrison, who generously made his collection of pictures and printed materials available to us.

Of enormous help was the excellent book, *Shark Point — High Point* (Tiburon-Belvedere), written by eighth graders at Reed School in 1954 and revised twice since then. This unique book is a treasure for which the entire community is indebted. Now out of print, it has become a rare book sought by collectors.

Other valuable sources were *The First Spanish Entry into San Francisco Bay*, Fred Stindt's history of the NWP, *Redwood Railways* by Gilbert Kneiss, and *Of Walking Beams and Paddlewheels* by George H. Harlan.

Most of all, we would like to thank those who have contributed photographs to the Landmarks Society's historical collection since it was organized twenty-five years ago, providing a rich body of material from which to choose. Especially valuable were the Reed family pictures, a bequest from the late Lucretia H. Little.

Finally, we are grateful to the Tiburon Centennial Committee, Branwell Fanning, chairman, and Denis Rice, publications committee chairman, for inaugurating this important project as part of the town's 100th birthday celebration.

The lithograph used in the cover design is from the collection of Joseph Baird, Jr.

All photographs unless otherwise credited are from the collection of the Landmarks Society of Tiburon & Belvedere.

Cover Design: Lawrence R. Peterson
Book Design: James Heig
Typesetting: Sherrell Graphics, San Francisco

First Edition
Copyright © 1984
Scottwall Associates
95 Scott Street
San Francisco, California 94117

Grateful acknowledgement is extended to John Howell Books, San Francisco, for permission to reprint excerpts from *The First Spanish Entry into San Francisco Bay, 1775,* copyright 1971, John Galvin, Editor, and to George H. Harlan and Clement Fisher, Jr., authors and publishers of *Of Walking Beams and Paddle Wheels,* copyright 1951, for permission to quote briefly and to use drawing for the endsheets of this book.

Printed in the United States of America.

ISBN 0-9612790-2-8 clothbound
ISBN 0-9612790-3-6 paperbound

Foreword

Tiburon never became a "Little Dublin" like San Francisco's populous South of the Slot district before the 1906 earthquake and fire. But the key protagonists in its early history were both Irishmen — John Reed and Peter Donahue.

These two men differed markedly from one another in background, talents and careers, but each was archetypical of his times and ideally equipped to seize advantage of the opportunities and potentials of the region in two radically different eras.

John Reed was one of these *Anglos* (to the Mexican-Californians, at least, who did not draw too fine a line between Celt and Anglo-Saxon) who integrated perfectly into the Hispanic ranching society of old Alta California. He then greased the way for such followers as the ex-whaler (like himself), William A. Richardson, who founded Sausalito a decade after Reed first squatted on its beach (1825), and Don Timoteo Murphy, who pioneered San Rafael after taking over from Reed as civilian major-domo of the secularized mission.

Reed, the first non-Hispanic to set roots deeply in Marin County, formally received his landgrant, *Rancho Corte Madera del Presidio*, in 1834. Through his wife, Hilaria, Reed had the right connections to prosper. His bride was the daughter of Alférez (Ensign) José Antonio Sánchez, later commandant of the San Francisco Presidio. Small wonder that Reed became a sort of small-scale Captain Sutter.

Peter Donahue was Reed's opposite, a man of urban, not rural life, of industry, not agriculture. Where Reed was "land-poor" (rich in acres, short on cash), Donahue was one of the wealthiest men in the entire West. Although appreciated by historians as the founder of railroads, a gas company and the Union Iron Works, he has been sold short by them. Actually, Donahue and his brothers loosed the Industrial Revolution upon the Pacific Coast. The sleepy pastoral society of Reed was ended by the Yankee know-how of the Irish immigrant.

Along the way, Donahue dragged Tiburon into the 20th Century — and as early as 1884. He founded the last real San Francisco Bay port there to connect his San Francisco and North Pacific Railroad, serving Marin and Sonoma Counties, with the Embarcadero by means of his small fleet of steamboats.

The subsequent history of Tiburon and its peninsula, of arks and yachts, dairy ranches, suburbs and commuters, is mundane stuff when compared to the tale of that first half-century of settlements, 1834-1884. For this reason, one of our main concerns today is connecting with that rich past which still enhances the present by a kind of magic. We do so by conserving the landscape that pleased the *ranchero*, Reed, like the unspoiled "island" of Ring Mountain, and by preserving the still-salvagable physical remains of Donahue's Industrial Revolution days, the cabin of the *China*, the Donahue Building of the railroad itself, and lovely old St. Hilary's.

We also cherish the more numerous, if evanescent, memories of olden times and manage to save the best of them in text and photograph in books of local history such as this one.

Tiburon is but a small peninsular point on the vast map of California, a nation among states. Yet, in its brief history of a century and a half as a recognizable geographical entity (and barely 100 years as a settlement), it has passed from a pastoral life, dating to ancient times, into a modern world that began with Donahue's "iron horses," walking beam engines, and double-enders. Its story is, thus, the history of the entire Far West, in a microcosm.

Richard Dillon

Preface

The Landmarks Society was organized to preserve Old St. Hilary's, the church built for the railroad workers in 1886, but the founders soon realized that it is not enough to save only a landmark. To preserve our heritage, there is need also to save the equally significant environment and the culture of the time and place.

The Society activities include historic publications, botanical and architectural tours, lectures, exhibits, collection of artifacts and fine art, archives of photographs and documents, research and reference library. Membership is open to anyone who is interested in local history and natural resources and who wishes to share in the responsibility of protecting the heritage of our communities.

By historic coincidence, 1984 is a landmark year: the 100th anniversary of the founding of Tiburon as a railroad town and the 20th anniversary of its incorporation, and the 25th anniversary of the Society, the first community historical organization in Marin County.

This year not only marks the periods of time passed, it is the beginning of a new historic era, the first time that the railroad will play no part, for the company has sold Point Tiburon. Upon the old railroad yard will rise new residential and retail buildings, modern landmarks.

The railroad has left and the only vestige of its hundred years is two landmarks, Old St. Hilary's and the terminal for train and ferry passengers, which was recently dubbed the Donahue Building. The Society maintains the Carpenter Gothic church and adjacent rare wildflower acreage. The Society expects to restore the Donahue Building to provide a community center for historic displays and archives and to create a working model of Point Tiburon circa 1900.

Landowners a century ago welcomed the railroad and the connecting ferry system because transportation would open the peninsula to a new diverse population, which certainly has come to be.

At the same time in the 19th century, photography was becoming commonplace, recording for the first time the events and personalities of the era, telling the story of ordinary work, play, and family life. For twenty-five years, photographs and documents have been collected by the Society through donations from local families and research in historical libraries. The archivist has established the system for salvaging, reproducing and protecting these fragile items from the deterioration of storage in attics and basements. The Society hopes to receive more records of the past and present in order to care for and catalog them for research, exhibits, and publication.

When the Tiburon Centennial Committee recommended the publication of a new book about Tiburon, the Landmarks Society conceived the centennial publication as a pictorial history of the area and residents before the railroad, the changes made by the railroad on the land and the lives of those it brought to the Tiburon peninsula, as well as the development during recent decades as the railroad withdrew.

From the treasures of the Landmarks Society, illustrations have been selected which give a fuller and more interesting record than could a volume of written text. Turn a page and the faces of the Reed family, which encouraged the building of the railroad, reflect the struggle with fortune and misfortune as they are caught between two cultures. Turn another page and all but hear the clamor of a steam shovel dumping the bluff of Point Tiburon into the railroad yard; turn another and be amused by thirteen stylish vacationers sitting with serene dignity in a rowboat that seems to be sinking under their weight. Continue and you will be struck by the disappearance of water and hillsides and the emergence of new land shown in a series of aerial photographs.

The unique geography of Point Tiburon projecting into San Francisco Bay attracted alike the Spanish explorers in the 18th century, the Yankee tycoons of the 19th century, and the real estate developers of the 20th century. Residents and visitors, in numbers no one could have foreseen a hundred years ago, have felt lucky to discover the place.

The Landmarks Society hopes that the centennial history book will provide an understanding of the development of the Tiburon Peninsula, the place of nature and the place of people, so that its special qualities will not be taken for granted, rather that its heritage will be protected, preserved, and where possible restored.

Beverly Bastian Meyers
Founder and Honorary President
Landmarks Society of Belvedere-Tiburon

Table of Contents

Pictorial History of
TIBURON

dess. et Lith. par Choris.

Lith. de Langlumé.

Coiffures de danse des habitans de la Californie.

This drawing, made by a Frenchman, Louis Choris, depicts natives he saw at Mission San Francisco de Asis (now called Mission Dolores) in 1816. Whether they are Miwoks no one can say, but many of this tribe were taken from Marin to be converted and to work in the mission fields. Some forty years before Choris, a Spanish priest describes his first encounter with Coast Miwoks on the Sausalito shore:

(Courtesy Bancroft Library)

The six others were young men of good presence and fine stature. Their colouring was not so weak as we have seen in Indians at Carmel. They were by no means filthy, and the best favoured were models of perfection; among them was a boy whose exceeding beauty stole my heart. One alone of the young men had several dark blue lines painted from the lower lip to the waist and from the left shoulder to the right, in such a way as to form a perfect cross. God grant that we may see them worshipping so sovereign an emblem.

Besides comely elegance of figure and quite faultless countenance there was also — as their chief adornment — the way they did up their long hair: after smoothing it well they stuck in it a four-toothed wooden comb and bound up the end in a net of cord and very small feathers that were dyed a deep red; and in the middle of the coiffure was tied a sort of ribbon, sometimes black, sometimes blue. Those Indians who did not arrange their hair in this fashion did it up in a club so as to keep it in a closely woven small net that seemed to be of hemp-like fibres dyed a dark blue.

— *Journal of Father Vicente Santa Maria, August, 1775*

The Natives of Tiburon Greet the Spaniards

"We cannibals must help these Christians."
— *Josephine Miles*

Native Americans have lived on the borders of San Francisco Bay for more than ten thousand years, as evidenced by the great shell mounds clustered around sheltered coves and estuaries of the bay. These mounds, which doubled as refuse heaps and burial grounds, were sometimes thirty feet high and a quarter mile long; they marked the sites of villages which the Spanish called *rancherias*. More than fifty of them are marked on a 1909 archeological map of the Tiburon peninsula, where permanent villages existed for at least three thousand years before the arrival of Europeans.

In 1967 the site of a Coast Miwok village was excavated off Blackfield Drive, in what is now Tiburon Hills, yielding bone whistles, cooking stones, mortars, scrapers, and sinkers, as well as a few arrow- and spearheads. The gentle aboriginal people who lived in that village have passed into memory, but these mute artifacts reveal much about their lives.

The mortars were used to grind acorns into a flour which, leached with water to remove the bitter taste, formed a staple of the Miwok diet. Cooking stones were heated over a fire, then dropped into a basket of flour and water and stirred to make a mush.

The sinkers may have been attached to fishing nets, skillfully woven of reeds or strips of hide. The scrapers were used to clean the skins of deer, bear and rabbit for use as blankets or cloaks thrown over the shoulders in cold weather. The bone whistles were used in the elaborate music and dance which were a vital part of tribal ritual.

Relatively few arrowheads were found; living so close to the bay, these people would have depended more on fish than on game. But they did hunt deer, carrying their flint-tipped arrows in quivers of rabbit fur, surprising their prey from ambush or wearing it down in a protracted chase. They may have obtained both the wood for the bows and the flint for the arrowheads by trading shells with inland tribes.

An 1859 map pinpoints a large shell mound on the west shore of Strawberry Point. The people of that village must

have seen an astonishing sight when the sun rose one morning in August, 1775: a Spanish ship, the *San Carlos,* anchored just off the Marin shore, probably near present-day Sausalito. Ancient rules of courtesy told the natives how to respond to this unprecedented event. They immediately gathered presents of food and valuable decorations, and took them to the shore to greet the visitors.

The ship's commander, Lt. Juan Manuel de Ayala, was under orders to explore and map San Francisco Bay, which had been discovered by a land expedition six years earlier. The ship's pilot, Jose Canizares, was dispatched with two crewmen in a longboat to take soundings and explore the bay's convoluted shoreline.

The young chaplain aboard the *San Carlos,* Father Vicente Santa Maria, wrote a detailed account of his encounters with the natives while the ship was anchored, first for a few days near Sausalito, then for a month on the north side of Angel Island, in the deep cove which now bears Lt. Ayala's name.

Father Vicente was fascinated by the natives, and describes them with compassion, objectivity, even humor. He sees them as individuals, and interprets their behavior on their own terms, rather than imposing a European's judgment of the "savages." In short, he sees the Miwoks as a civilized people with a complex culture which he attempts to understand. Such qualities make him unique among early explorers of California.

Vicente, a Spaniard, had been trained as a missionary at the Franciscan Seminary in Mexico. After six years in the New World, he was eager to make converts, not to serve as ship's chaplain, and, as was later said of him, he "was not exactly one for being kept in hand." While his companions explored the bay, the 33-year-old padre spent much of his time pacing the deck of the San Carlos, waiting for the launch to return so that he could use it to visit the aborigines, who were gesturing madly from the shore and stepping in front of their arrows to show their friendliness.

(Photo: Gerrie Reichard)

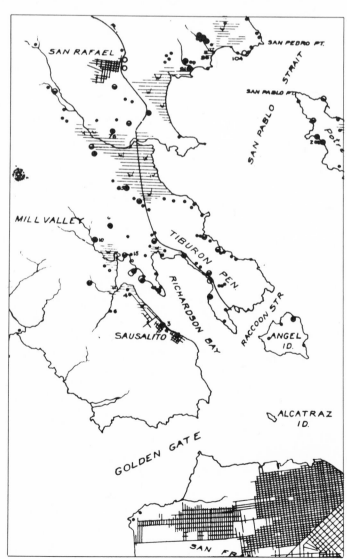

At Ring Mountain, a large nature preserve on the north-east shore of the Tiburon peninsula, this large rock shows evidence of the people who flourished here ages ago: several dozen petroglyphs, oval or circular grooves carved into the stone thousands of years ago, in clusters, at a height appropriate to human hands. Their meaning seems to be symbolic rather than pictorial. Scientists have conjectured that women carved the circles, perhaps to insure their own or the earth's fertility. Similar marks have been found elsewhere in Marin and Sonoma Counties. These were noticed only a few years ago.

A portion of "Map of the San Francisco Bay Region Showing Distribution of Shell Heaps" (1909) identifies more than fifty sites on the Tiburon peninsula where natives lived in permanent villages. Larger dots, indicating major sites, appear on Strawberry Point, the north end of Belvedere, and the west shore of Tiburon. Richardson Bay could certainly be the "large round cove" where Father Vicente Santa Maria and crewmen from the San Carlos visited a village as honored guests. Survey maps made in 1859 and 1869 both show an "Indian Mound" on the round knob which projects from the west shore of Strawberry, and another on the ridge above Mill Valley. These could have been the villages of natives who worked for John Reed in the 1830's.

After the arrival of the Spaniards in California (1769) and the establishment of the missions, the people of the coastal tribes were taken, often by force, to be converted to Christianity and to work for their salvation and their daily bread in the mission fields and orchards. More than two thousand Coast Miwok people — about two thirds of the entire aboriginal population — were baptized in the four nearest missions, San Rafael, San Francisco, Sonoma, and San Jose. The minority who eluded capture were utterly without rights or protection. Most of the villages were abandoned.

As Spanish, Mexican, and European settlers obtained land grants, a few *rancherias* were spared. On the Tiburon peninsula, a group of Coast Miwoks lived in their old village and worked for pioneer settler John Reed on his *Rancho Corte Madera* in the 1830's, tending his herds in return for his support and protection.

The native people, having no immunity to diseases brought by white men, succumbed to consumption, measles, "brain fever," and syphilis; indeed, Mission San Rafael was founded as a hospital for ailing "neophytes" (native converts) who had become ill in the chilly fogs at the San Francisco Mission. The first priest there had even evolved a method of performing caesarian sections in order to save the babies of syphilitic mothers. But nothing could protect against the worst scourge of all: smallpox. In the epidemic of 1838, an estimated forty to seventy thousand natives died in the region north of San Francisco Bay.

The few who survived to see the Yankee immigration in the 1840's may well have regretted their luck. While the Spaniards and Mexicans captured and virtually enslaved many thousands of natives, they did regard them as human, and thus as worthy of salvation. The Yankees, who had fought the fiercer tribes of the plains and mountains on the way west, generally regarded the "Diggers," as they called them, as subhuman, worthy only of extermination.

Today, just two centuries after the arrival of white men, only mortars and cooking stones and a few mysterious petroglyphs speak of a culture otherwise erased from the earth.

Another drawing by Louis Choris, from his 1816 expedition, shows two bird hunters (are those quail on the ground near the quiver?) against a background which looks decidedly familiar. The authenticity of this drawing has been questioned; critics have said that natives of the bay area did not use bows and arrows, that the vegetation looks tropical, and that the scene could be Polynesian. But these men have coiffures and physiques exactly like those described by Father Vicente in his journal; arrowheads were found in a dig on the Tiburon peninsula, and the plants at left could be sword ferns — or just artistic license.

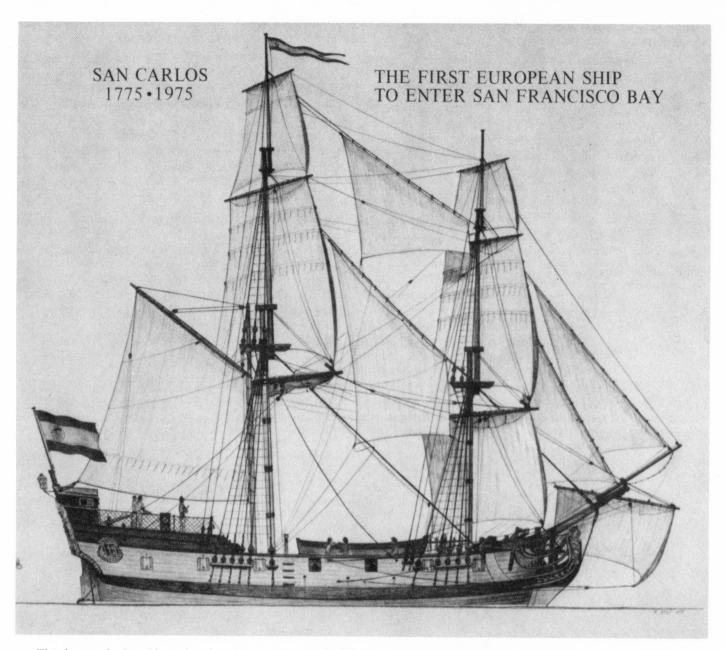

SAN CARLOS
1775•1975

THE FIRST EUROPEAN SHIP
TO ENTER SAN FRANCISCO BAY

This drawing by Ray Aker is based on three years' research of documents from the 1700's, including exhaustive inventories of the ship's movable and immovable parts. The San Carlos was slightly over eighty feet long, with a breadth of twenty feet, and carried a longboat of twenty-one feet.

— Courtesy National Maritime Museum, San Francisco

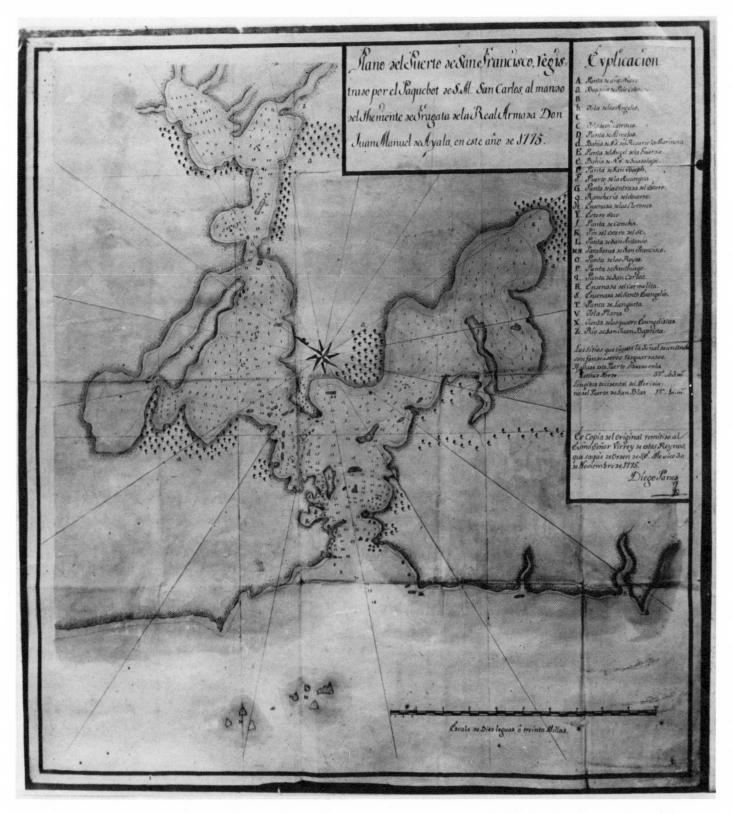

Here is the map drawn by Jose Canizares and the crew of the San Carlos, who spent more than a month taking soundings and exploring the far reaches of the bay. The "Explicacion" shows "b. Isla de los Angeles" (Angel Island) and "c. Isla de Alcatraces" (Island of the Pelicans), the only two names which have come down to the present day. "Isla de Alcatraces" is, however, not the present Alcatraz but Yerba Buena Island. How the name was shifted after this map was drawn is a mystery.

(Courtesy Bancroft Library)

THE JOURNAL OF FATHER VICENTE SANTA MARIA, 1775

Today the captain decided to go to an island that we called Santa María de los Angeles. This was done, and when the ship was anchored again we went ashore to reconnoiter the island terrain.

With one sailor along, I was foremost in making a diversion of this duty, in hopes of coming upon Indians. All afternoon of the 14th I wore myself out at it. On the pitch of a hill slope I discovered two huts, certainly Indian lodgings though deserted. I went near them, and seeing them unoccupied I was minded to take the path to a spring of fresh water, to quench a burning thirst brought on as much by the great seasonal heat as by the hard work of climbing up and down such rugged high hills. In a short while I came to a large rock with a cleft in the middle of it, in which rested three remarkable droll objects, and I was led to wonder if they were likeness of some idol that the Indians reverenced.

These were slim round shafts about a yard and a half high, ornamented at the top with bunches of white feathers, and ending, to finish them off, in an arrangement of black and red-dyed feathers imitating the appearance of a sun. They even had, as their drollest adornment, pieces of the little nets with which we had seen the Indians cover their hair.

At the foot of this niche were many arrows with their tips stuck in the ground as if symbolizing abasement. This last exhibit gave me the unhappy suspicion that those bunches of feathers representing the image of the sun (which in their language they call *gisman*) must be objects of the Indians' heathenish veneration; and if this was true — as was a not unreasonable conjecture — these objects suffered a merited penalty in being thrown on the fire. After spending several days in going over other parts of this island I came upon two rancherías with no one in them. I inferred that they served as shelters to Indians when they came there to hunt deer, which are the most numerous animals on the island.

It would be about 10 o'clock in the forenoon of the 23rd of August when, towards the point of the Isla de Santa María de los Angeles near which we stayed, two reed boats were seen approaching, in which were five Indians. As soon as the captain was informed of this, he directed that signs be made inviting them aboard, to which they promptly responded by coming, which was what they wanted to do. Leaving their boats, they climbed aboard quite fearlessly. They were in great delight, marvelling at the structure of the ship, their eyes fixed most of all on the rigging. They wondered no less at the lambs, hens, and pigeons that were providently kept to meet our needs if someone on board should fall sick. But what most captivated and pleased them was the sound of the ship's bell, which was purposely ordered to be struck so we could see what effect it had on ears that had never heard

it. It pleased the Indians so much that while they were on board they went up to it from time to time to sound it themselves. They brought us, as on other occasions, gifts of pinoles, and they even remembered men's names that we had made known to them earlier.

Word of the kindliness with which those on the ship dealt with these heathen was spread so quickly from ranchería to ranchería that it served to dispel the fears of a number of Indians not hitherto seen by us, so that they hastened to come aboard. They came, at the same time, to offer us (perhaps depriving themselves) the food of their daily sustenance. This event, which set before our eyes a new spectacle, took place that same day, the 24th of August, two and a half hours after those Indians I have just told about had gone away. These others came in two balsas and numbered about eight in all. When they were in sight close by, and we made signs to them to come to the ship, one of them, who doubtless came to the bow of his boat for the purpose, began to make a long speech, giving us to understand that it was the head man of the ranchería who came, and that he was at our service. This visit was not a casual one, for all of them appeared to have got themselves up, each as best he could, for a festive occasion. Some had adorned their heads with a tuft of red-dyed feathers, and others with a garland of them mixed with black ones. Their chests were covered with a sort of woven jacket made with ash-coloured feathers; and the rest of their bodies, though bare, was all worked over with various designs in charcoal and red ochre, presenting a droll sight.

As soon as they left their boats, it was made clear to them who it was that commanded the ship, and they endeavoured to point out their leader to us. The chieftain of the ranchería had all his men, one after another, in the order of their importance, salute our captain; and when this ceremony was completed he begged us all to sit down, as the Indians also did, for distribution among us of their offering, which they brought to us in all tidiness. All being in their places in due order, the second chieftain, who was among the company, asked of another Indian a container made of reeds that he carried with him, in which were many pats or small cakes of pinole. It was given him, and having placed it beside him he indicated that he was to be listened to. With no lack of self-composure he spoke for quite a while, and then, opening the container, handed the pinole cakes to the first chieftain, who as soon as he received them handed them to our captain, making signs to him to distribute them among all the men of the ship, insisting, moreover, that he be the first to taste the pinole. The second chieftain was now very watchful to see if by chance anyone of the ship's company had missed partaking of the bread of hospitality; he went up to the roundhouse, and several times stuck his head in the after

This excerpt from Father Vicente Santa Maria's journal, beginning with the arrival of the San Carlos at Angel Island and sampling the events of several ensuing days, shows the lively style, acute observation, and humane attitude which make his writing a delight. The natives described are certainly from the Tiburon peninsula.

hold; there was no limit to his painstaking inspection. After this our captain directed the steward to bring some pieces of pilot bread and gave them to the Indian head man, who distributed them with all formality among his party.

The eight Indians who came to us on this occasion were named as follows: their chieftain was called *Sumu*; the second chieftain, *Jausos*; the others, *Supitacse* (1); *Tilasce* (2); *Mutuc* (3); *Logeacse* (4); *Guecpostole* (5); *Xacacse* (6). To give an example of Jausos' liveliness: on being taught to say "piloto Cañizares," he made signs that Sumu be taught to say the same thing. When Sumu mistakenly said "pinoto" instead of "piloto," Jausos corrected him, laughing so hard as to astonish all of us. They are very fond of trading. All of them hanker for our clothes, our cloaks most of all, and so as to move us to make them warm they show us with sad gestures how they suffer from the cold and even say the words *coroec cata*, "I am cold," and the like.

Soon after these Indians came to the ship there came eight others of our new friends, and at first it appeared that those of the one and the other ranchería did not look on each other with much friendliness, but our treating them all as equals made them friends and on speaking terms with one another.

We taught all of them how to cross themselves; and although those who came under Sumu's command were better disposed toward these pious observances, the In-dians who came under the command of the other ranchería's head man became compliant, and all of them came to me to be instructed. Among all these Indians Mutuc is noticeably clever, so perceptive that he not only grasped at once what we said to him in Spanish, and repeated it exactly, but also, as if well versed in our language, he showed how the Spanish terms we asked about were expressed in his. On this day it came off colder than usual, and of the poor unfortunates on board those who could do so took refuge under my cloak, showing with piteous looks how keenly, being stark naked, they felt the chill. Luck, it seems, offered a sailor's long coat to Supitacse, the oldest and least forward of them all, as soon as he came on board, and he took it at once and kept himself warm in it, huddling in corners. When it was time to leave, he most considerately put the garment back where he had taken possession of it. True, the first day that Sumu's party came aboard, most of his Indians, especially Jausos and one other, were somewhat troublesome because they had a fancy for everything. Everything looked good to them and they all wanted to barter with their feathers and little nets, but once we had given them to understand that this was doing wrong they behaved quite differently thereafter, so that two who had been wandering all over the ship did not now leave my side unless they were called. This was a striking example of how tractable they were.

August, 1775

Another drawing by Louis Choris (1816) shows natives in a tule boat exactly like those described by Father Vicente Santa Maria. Elliott Evans, in "Chronology of Angel Island," credits this drawing as "the first representation of Angel Island," with Point Blunt in the background. (Courtesy Bancroft Library)

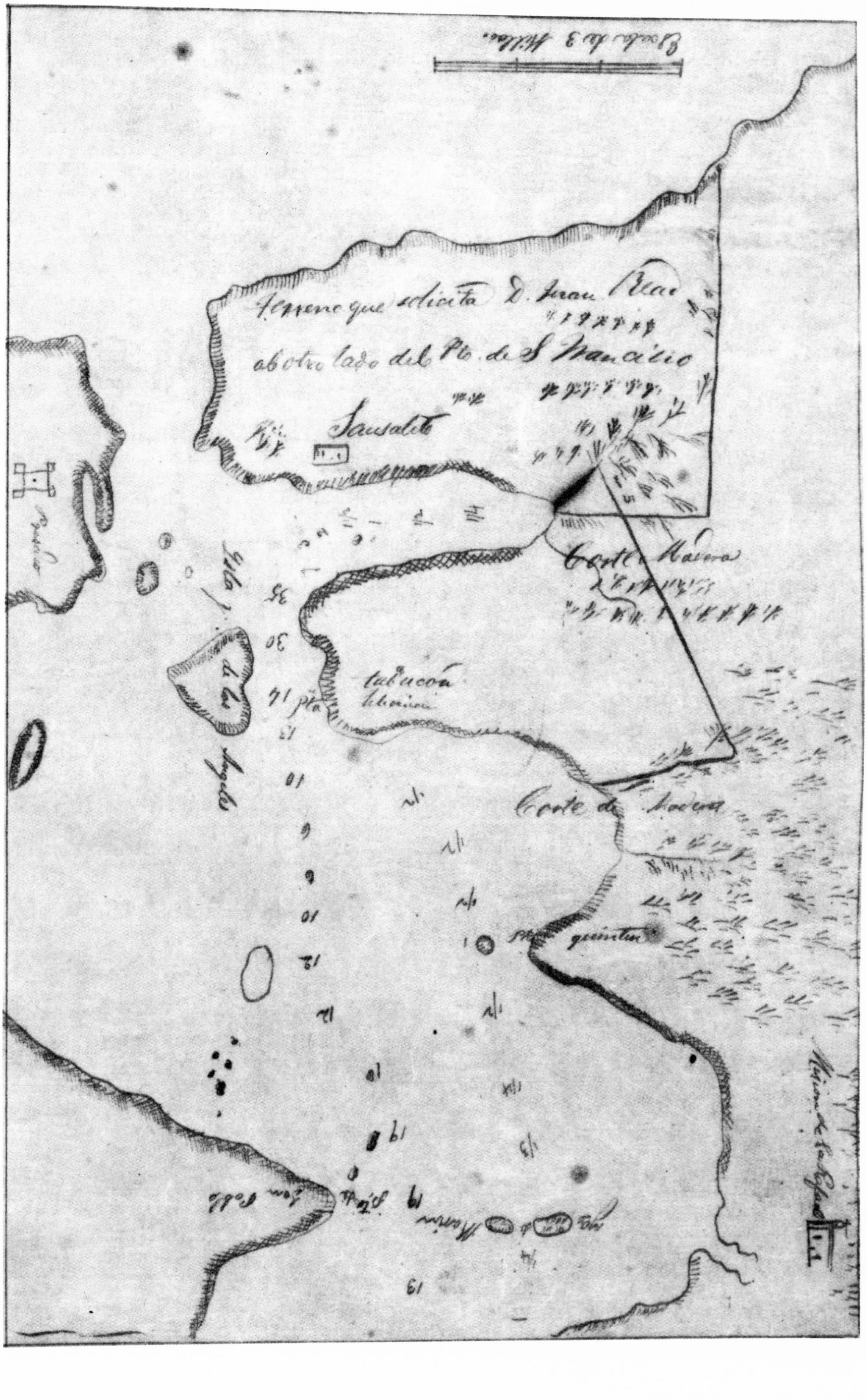

Escala de 3 Millas.

Terreno que solicita D. Juan Read
ab otro lado del P.° de S. Mauricio
Sausalito

Corte de Madera

Corte de Madera

quintin

Pta de Angel

tuburón

Puebla

John Thomas Reed, Pioneer

The Irishman known as John Reed was not only the first settler on the Tiburon Peninsula, but the first European settler in Marin County. His story has drawn enormous interest from historians and laymen alike down through the years, yet much of it remains a mystery.

We know nothing about his early life and family except that he was born in Dublin in 1805 and left for Mexico fifteen years later with an uncle. He spent the next five years there, apparently serving as a seaman on a whaling ship out of Acapulco.

We don't even know what he looked like (although a legend handed down gives him blond hair and blue eyes), because he died in 1842, before the newly-invented art of photography reached this coast.

He left us no word of what it was like — to arrive, a man just out of his teens, in this remote province; to work from first light to after dark, day after day, year after year, carving a vast cattle rancho from the Marin wilderness; to live as a Mexican Don in a primitive country, with children who were strangers to the English tongue and a shy young wife who could not write her own name.

What follows is what we do know, an account pieced together from the facts that have come to light from land grant records, the diaries of other people, and the slender extant historical records.

* * *

Reed first set foot on the Marin peninsula in 1825, when his whaling ship stopped at Sausalito for water and he took "French leave," the usual way for foreigners to enter California in those days. He was young, this sailor, but he was already obsessed by what was then the California Dream: to have a modest plot of land — four or five thousand acres —

Opposite: This drawing accompanied John Reed's petition for a grant to the Rancho Corte de Madera del Presidio in 1834. It shows Reed's house at Sausalito, where he lived while ferrying fresh water to the Presidio, at upper left. Angel Island is heart-shaped. "Pta. Tiburon" has "tabucon" written above it, perhaps in a later hand. "Pta. Quintin" and Mision de San Rafael are at lower right, opposite "Pta. de San Pablo."

cattle, horses to ride, a pretty senorita to cook his frijoles, and a dozen children to carry on his name.

Reed's fluent Spanish, his knowledge of Mexican customs, and the fact that he was already a Catholic (required for citizenship, and only citizens could own land) gave him an advantage over his fellow foreigners, who knew neither the language nor the customs of the country. He had only to find the land he wanted, build a house and occupy it for a year, and undergo the formality of becoming a naturalized Mexican citizen.

To his dismay, Reed discovered that nearly all the land around the bay was taken up by the missions or by the cattle ranches of the Mexican soldiers. Except for the seacoast and the headlands, what is now Marin County belonged to the San Rafael Mission. When Reed asked for a grant to Sausalito and was refused (the government wanted it to remain in military hands), he had to look further north — all the way to what is now Sonoma County.

This was rash of him. That region was not entirely unpopulated in 1826; there were Russian fur-trappers on the coast and San Francisco de Solano Mission inland, but in between were Indian tribes so hostile that the padre at Sonoma seldom went more than a hundred yards from the mission compound except under heavy guard. Despite a strong warning from Father Juan Amoros at Mission San Rafael, who reluctantly gave him the cattle and farm implements he would need to get started, Reed built a tule hut near the Kotati village where the town of Cotati is today, and planted grain.

That was the year a gang of annoyed converts and their outside accomplices burned down part of the Sonoma Mission and made off with the harvest. Reed was lucky. Although he had increased the provocation by settling on the main Indian trail to the Bodega clam beds, the natives merely burnt his crop, pulled down his hut, and killed his cattle.

Temporarily cured of his fever for land at any cost, he returned to Sausalito, where he built a wooden shanty and made a living for a few years dipping fresh water from a hillside creek and rowing it across the bay for sale to the soldiers and their families at the San Francisco Presidio. Since

The ruins of John Reed's adobe, built in 1836 near La Goma and Locke Lane, Mill Valley; this picture was taken in 1916.

he also took passengers on occasion, his little business is regarded as the first ferry service on San Francisco Bay.

In 1831, six long years after his arrival in California, Reed finally succeeded in obtaining provisional permission to occupy the *Rancho Corte de Madera del Presidio,* a vast tract of redwood groves and golden grassland that spread out from the Tiburon peninsula to Mill Valley and as far up as the San Quentin sloughs. In former years the mission cattle had grazed there.

Reed began with 400 cattle and 60 horses, some of them given to him by Father Amoros in 1831. He put up fences and planted fruit trees. Since the native cows were scrawny, horned beasts who would give milk only if they could be caught and tied down, he sent to England for dairy cows, a novelty in Mexican California. He also cut firewood for sale to the soldiers at the Presidio ("Corte Madera" is Spanish for "place where wood is cut.")

When the rancho was formally granted to "Citizen Don Juan Reed" in 1834, he "pulled up various herbs and stones and threw them to the four winds in sign of his legal and legitimate possession." It was only a tradition, but perhaps it brought luck: although the boundaries were not finally settled until the 1880's, Reed's would turn out to be one of the few California land grant titles about which there was virtually no dispute.

In 1836 he built a sawmill in what is now Mill Valley and began logging the towering redwoods there. The remains of this mill are preserved as a state historical landmark in Old Mill Park.

That same year, Reed realized the rest of his dream. In a ceremony held October 12 at Mission Dolores, he married Hilaria Sanchez, the youngest daughter of Jose Antonio

Sanchez, the *alferez* (later *commandante*) at the San Francisco Presidio. She was 23, he 31.

Reed was for a time administrator of Mission San Rafael, which, like all the missions, was being closed down. His job, which included overseeing the distribution of mission property to the emancipated converts, lasted just five months, from November 30, 1836, until April 21, 1837, when he was replaced by another Irishman, Don Timoteo Murphy.

Reed returned to Mill Valley and either began or resumed building a two-story adobe house there, hiring skilled Indians from Sutter's Fort to help him. His first child, John Joseph Reed, was born July 16, 1837. Perhaps in celebration, the new father, a devout Catholic, climbed up Mount Tamalpais and placed on its summit a wooden cross that could be seen all the way to the Farallones.

Hilaria had three more children: Richard, born around 1839, Hilarita in 1840, and Maria Inez in 1842. (Richard died at the age of twelve.)

By 1841, Don Juan Reed had about 2,000 head of cattle, 200 horses, and 1,000 sheep. In that year, a good two-year-old cow sold for $4.00, and a calf for $1.50. The present Belvedere Island was Reed's potrero, or pasture, for fattening cattle, with a crude fence across the causeway to keep the livestock in. Rodeos were held there when the cattle were ready for slaughter. Reed kept salt yards, a brickyard, and even a stone quarry, as well as herds of cattle on the Tiburon Peninsula.

These were the good days, when the land effortlessly produced all a man could want, and his herds thrived on the plentiful grasses, increasing by one-third every year despite the depredations of wolves, coyotes, and bears. Not even the irritating proximity of William Antonio Richardson, an

10

Englishman who had acquired title to the Sausalito grant in 1836 and come to live on it in 1841, could disturb Reed in the enjoyment of what he had worked so hard to achieve in this foreign land.

Or did he enjoy it? French visitor Duflot de Mofras, who claimed to know him well, maintained that Reed was so discouraged by the many hardships of his life that he would have liked nothing better than to sell his lands and leave California.

Whether this was true or not, it could not have been an easy existence. In April, 1837, Philip L. Edwards, a native of Kentucky who had come down from Oregon with some companions to buy cattle, visited Reed's rancho and professed himself charmed by his surroundings:

> . . . As I sat in a house of antique construction, looked upon the primitive manners of the father [Quijas, a dissolute but well-liked padre from Mission San Rafael], the unaffected hospitality of our hostess and the convivial hilarity of all, feudal recollections passed rapidly through my mind. I felt myself transported back to former centuries and mingling in the transactions of an age that is past. Truly this people [the Spanish] seemed to be, as Santa Anna said of them, "a century behind the rest of Christendom."

Yet Edwards also mentions that on the way to the rancho,

the tide being low, "a part of us were forced to land and walk about 4 miles," reaching the adobe after dark. There were few books, few social gatherings, little indeed to break the monotony of a life where each day was just like the one that came before.

In December, 1841, another Yankee, a Bostonian named Henry Peirce, went with Reed to view the old mission and then passed a night at the Mill Valley rancho, trying to sleep despite the baying of his host's English hounds. His diary gives us another glimpse of life at the Reed Adobe:

> We arrived at Mr. Reed's, drenched to the skin, just as darkness set in. Entering the house, we met a person [Padre Quijas] draped in the coarse grey habit of a Dominican priest; he was very drunk, and embraced each of us in the affectionate manner of Spanish people.
>
> It was sometime before Mr. Reed entered the house. When he did, he informed us that he had been absent searching the woods for his wife, who had fled there to avoid the insults and beastly conduct that the priest had exhibited toward her just previous to our arrival."

It was living "a century behind the rest of Christendom" that killed John Reed. In June of 1842, he toppled from his horse, a victim of sunstroke. (Hilaria's own testimony is the source for this date.) His friends knew enough about blood-

The oldest photograph in the Landmarks Society collection is this daguerreotype of Hilaria Sanchez Reed and her son John Joseph, taken in the early 1850's, when he was about fourteen years old.

John Joseph Reed in his early 30's, tall, prosperous, and with a gold watch fob, circa 1870.

letting to open his veins, but not enough to close them again, and he bled to death at the age of 37. He was buried at the Catholic cemetery in San Rafael.

Like most young women in California, his 29-year-old widow, Hilaria, was illiterate, and could neither speak nor understand English. She and her four small children owned miles of land, and thousands of cattle, sheep, and horses, but they could not get on without help. The land grant records mention that a sea captain named J.J. Papys became guardian of the children, and was promised part of the rancho as compensation, but this arrangement remains mysterious.

Three years after her husband's death, Hilaria married her first cousin, 24-year-old Bernardino Garcia, who had served as a soldier in Vallejo's company in Sonoma. He and Hilaria had three children, two girls and then a boy; only one daughter, Carmelita, survived.

Garcia is a notorious character in California history. He is blamed for the savage murder of two captured Americans during the Bear Flag Revolt in June, 1846, an act which turned what had been little more than a comic farce into a bitter skirmish between the Americans and Californians. Later, he was to achieve fame as "Three-Fingered Jack," a ruffian in Joaquin Murietta's band. Garcia was shot and killed in 1853 by a Texas bounty hunter named Captain Harry Love, who cut off his victim's hand to prove he was indeed Three-Fingered Jack.

The Heirs

The family John Reed left behind when he died would make fine subjects for a romantic novel, were there not so many gaps in their history.

In 1868, Hilaria Reed Garcia died and the rancho was divided among her three surviving Reed children.

John Joseph Reed (1837-1899)

John Reed's oldest son was given the lion's share, more than 2000 acres comprising the upper portion of the Tiburon Peninsula.

He seems to have lived away from home for most of his childhood, perhaps in Mexico with his great-uncle. We know that he attended school at Mission Dolores in San Francisco. He returned to the rancho in 1859, when he was 22, and fathered a child. Clotilde, born that year, was declared John Joseph's legal child and subsequently raised by the Reeds. Although the baby's mother, Barbara Sibrian, never married John Joseph, she was accepted as a member of the family. She later married a man named Vidal, and lived at Pacheco and Hancock.

John Joseph married Carlota Suarez, a girl from Mazatlan, Mexico, probably in the 1860's. Clotilde's half-brother, John Paul Reed, was born in 1865. The two children were given their own livestock and trained in the business of managing a ranch.

In 1876 John Joseph and Carlota built a fourteen-room white mansion near what is now Bel Aire. Although their house was distinctly American in design, its occupants were decidedly Latin. Everybody in the family spoke Spanish as his first language, and they corresponded in that language until the end of their lives.

Carlota and John Joseph continued the old Spanish tradition of hospitality, entertaining their many friends and relatives at large parties, often with music, very much like the fandangos of the early 1800's, and maintained close friendships with old Californio families in Contra Costa and Alameda Counties.

Maria Inez Reed (1841-1883)

Inez, who had married Pennsylvania native Thomas Deffebach, a printer, in 1864, was allotted the smallest (646 acres) but probably most valuable portion of the rancho, since it included the Reed adobe and the future town of Mill Valley. The Deffebachs had eleven children, only four of whom survived to adulthood.

Hilarita Reed (1839-1908)

Hilarita Reed, a capable woman who had her own herd and a registered brand for her cattle, fell heir to the lower portion of the Tiburon peninsula (1020 acres) and Strawberry Point (446 acres). Belvedere was not finally recognized as part of the Reed estate until 1883.

In 1872 she married Canadian-born Dr. Benjamin Lyford,

This remarkable group portrait shows Inez and Hilarita Reed (standing) with their half-sister, Carmelita Garcia (seated, right) and Barbara Sibrian, the unwed mother of Clotilde Reed, in the early 1860's.

The girls wear hoop skirts and cinched-in waists fashionable at the time of the Civil War; belt buckles, brooches and earrings indicate their social standing. Barbara Sibrian was clearly accepted as a member of the Reed family; her daughter would be three or four years old. Why didn't John Joseph marry her?

The rigid poses and staring eyes result from the necessity of holding perfectly still — and not blinking — for several seconds.

Clotilde and John Paul Reed in an ambrotype made about 1869, when she was ten and he six.

who had come to California after serving as "an embalming surgeon" in the Civil War. A photograph taken on the battlefield shows him outside his embalming tent, with obviously live soldiers posed as corpses in coffins and on an operating table in front.

Lyford had very strong ideas about sanitation, morality, and health. Arrested during the war for appearing in a brothel in uniform, he protested heatedly that he had "not once during my life patronized a house of that kind" . . . that he held "such habits in the most supreme contempt." He claimed he had gone into the house only to look for someone (a steamboat clerk). This sounds like a familiar excuse; in Lyford's case it was probably true.

He began practising medicine in San Francisco in 1866 but switched to the dairy business a few years after his marriage. He and Hilarita and John Joseph operated four dairies on the Tiburon peninsula, hiring Portuguese and Italian immigrants to do the work. Lyford's Eagle Dairy exemplified his ideals of health and cleanliness.

Lyford continued to experiment with embalming techniques. His laboratory was a small building made from the cabin of a dismantled ship. It is clearly visible just beside the

Clotilde Reed (1859-1940). This beautiful portrait may be a graduation picture, taken about 1876, when she was sixteen; no date is given. An inscription tells us that the dress is white silk, with pale blue ribbons; earrings "little diamonds" in gold, a gold hair ornament; the medals are all silver except the cross, which is gold. Clearly she is somebody's darling, a young lady for whom nothing is too good. John Joseph had her declared his legal daughter, and raised her himself; very likely he could not bear to let her go when her mother married and moved away. She in turn was a dutiful daughter, devoted to him and her stepmother. Both pictures on this page are by Edouart & Cobb, 504 Kearny Street, San Francisco.

John Paul Reed (1865-1919). His mustache is as yet just a shadow, his clear gaze reflects the optimism of perhaps seventeen years, dating this picture about 1882. The pedestal, with incised decoration, was probably the latest thing. A gold watch with fob and chain was often a graduation present; the books too suggest such an occasion.

Lyford house in an early picture (pg. 124). He successfully embalmed a body for transportation across the sea, but his formula was lost when he died (June 13, 1906). The Lyfords were childless but they raised three children of Inez and Thomas Deffebach, who died early, in 1883 and 1885.

Carmelita Natividad Garcia (1845-1906)

Hilaria Reed's daughter by Garcia, Carmelita Natividad, was raised with her half-sisters, Hilarita and Inez; by all accounts she was very beautiful. In 1863 she married Hugh Boyle, a native of Missouri, who also went into dairying on the rancho.

Clotilde Reed (1859-1940)

Clotilde never married, but remained with her father and her stepmother until their deaths in 1899 and 1913, respectively. We see her in picture after picture, slim and elegantly dressed, gazing out at us with a serene, self-confident, aloof expression. After her stepmother's death, she divided her time between Tiburon and Alameda.

John Paul Reed (1865-1919)

John Paul never married either. Rather short and stocky, he wore a very full mustache that makes him easy to pick out in the old pictures. He lived with his parents until their deaths, then remained on the ranch until his own death.

Carlota Suarez, of Mazatlan, Mexico, married John Joseph around 1860.

A fiesta at the Reed ranch in the early 1890's featured three guitars and plenty of polka-dots. John Paul, tanned and happy, and Clotilde, more somber, sit in front of their parents. Carlota has aged visibly. John Joseph looks young and fit, with no grey in his hair. A young lady in flowered dress and hat rests her hands lightly on his shoulder. She is Frances Cora Laurence, whose day is coming.

A rather more formal party at the Reed ranch house, circa 1893, with a small orchestra (harp, violin, flute). John Paul and his parents are at center; Clotilde, in white, just above her stepmother. The house, originally a fine Greek Revival Style built in the 1870's, was enlarged some ten years later to fourteen rooms. The older section had eight panes per window, the newer only two. Some sixty-five years after the party above, the house (left) waits for demolition, in 1959, to make way for a modern residence. Today it would surely be rescued.

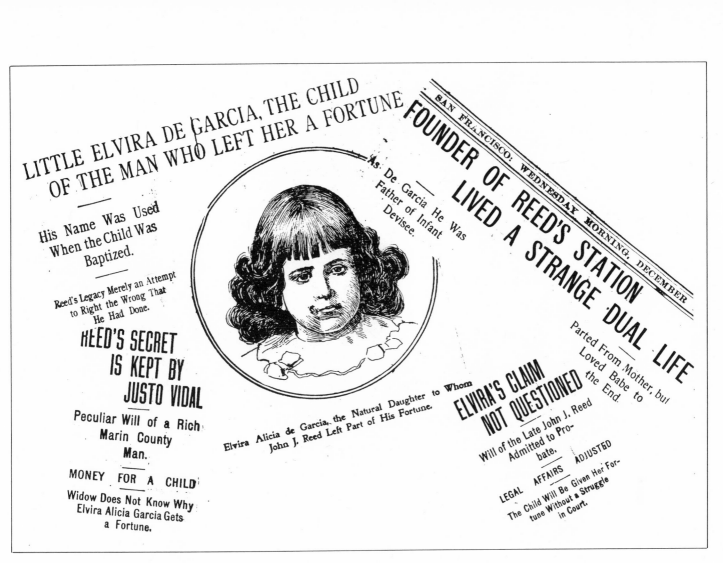

The newspapers loved scandal, and squeezed every drop from this story.

Elvira Alice Reed

John Joseph Reed died at home on December 1, 1899, leaving his widow, Carlota, and his two grown children, Clotilde and John Paul, the bulk of his $150,000 estate. But there was one very surprising bequest. Property worth about $25,000, including one hundred acres of land at El Campo, was to go to one Elvira Alice de Garcia, age six.

"It is all a mystery," Carlotta Reed told an *Examiner* reporter. "In the years I was his wife, and down to the very end, Mr. Reed never mentioned any de Garcia woman or child."

Within twenty-four hours after the will was read, reporters had traced the child's mother, "a frail little woman, pale and haggard," to her flat on Buchanan Street and wrung the story out of her.

Her name was Frances Cora Laurence. Orphaned at the age of eleven, around 1880, she had come to live with Carmelita and Hugh Boyle in Mill Valley. Naturally, she often met Carmelita's half-brother, John Joseph, then approaching 50. "I grew up with Reed continually about me," Frances told a reporter, "I learned to love him and I knew my love was returned."

In June, 1893, Frances Laurence moved to San Francisco, taking the name "de Garcia." Six months later she gave birth to a daughter.

Reed often came to see the little girl, christened Elvira Alice Reed, and he paid the bills for the house on Buchanan Street. The baby had the creamy skin and glossy black hair of her grandmother, Hilaria Sanchez, and the dark-blue eyes of her mother.

Three years later, Frances married an Englishman, J.C. Wood, and both mother and daughter took the name Wood. Reed's visits all but stopped; it was said that he never forgave his mistress for this marriage. Wood died while on a visit to England in 1898.

Reed went to San Francisco to see his daughter in October, 1899. On November 25, six days before his death, he called his lawyer into his bedroom and dictated the change in his will that would make front page news in the San Francisco papers before a fortnight had passed.

The will was not contested. At age 21, Elvira came into her legacy. She was also one of the beneficiaries of the estate of Clotilde Reed, who died in 1940.

Above: Hilarita Reed Lyford travelled with her husband to Washington and Philadelphia to see the Centennial Exhibition in 1876; they chose furnishings and pictures for their beautiful new house on Strawberry Point.

The Reed Legacy to Tiburon

Anyone driving through the Tiburon peninsula today will see dozens of reminders of the Reed family. Streets, circles, schools and subdivisions were named for various members of the family, and St. Hilary's churches (old and new) were named for Hilaria's patron saint. Mill Valley and Corte Madera are names derived from John Reed's earlier occupations. Even the unwed mother of Clotilde, Barbara Sibrian, is commemorated in the name of a 1983 subdivision (variant spelling Cibrian).

It is good that the Reed name is so liberally sprinkled over the landscape of southern Marin, because it has not survived as a surname; the only present-day members of the family are descended through Inez and Carmelita — and through Elvira de Garcia, the little girl John Joseph remembered in his will.

SITUATED as this dairy is in direct proximity to the celebrated "Tiburon Tract" and being also a part of the Rancho Corte de Madera del Presidio, it is eminently fitting that we give a description of those advantages which have gained for it the name of the Model Dairy of California. Many years ago Dr. Lyford, its founder, conceived the project of establishing a dairy which should not only be the *ne plus ultra* of perfection, but beyond all possibility of imitation. He selected the beautiful spot shown in the photo-engraving on back cover. The dairy house is located to the windward, so that all unpleasant odors and unhealthy air are carried towards the ocean, never reaching the dairy. A choice head of Jersey cows were selected by Dr. Lyford, and a full outfit of mechanical and chemical apparatus for testing and manufacturing butter was procured at great expense. The characteristics of Dr. Lyford's dairy are and ever have been, absolute cleanliness, the most skilled butter makers, the best cared for and the best fed cows. Hence the butter is the pure, unadulterated article.

The entire system is in accordance with the following code of requirements that Dr. Lyford has concluded as necessary to the proper conduct of the dairy:

1. The choicest interbred Jersey cows.
2. The choicest dairy feed for cows.
3. The choicest attention and guarantee against diseased cows.
4. The choicest attention and guarantee as to absolute cleanliness.
5. The choicest mechanical and chemical perfected dairy premises.
6. The most skilled butter maker and assistants and a positive demand to use absolute kindness to all dairy cows, consequently attendancy to the scientific conditions, all of which are absolutely necessary to the perfect production of milk, cream and butter.

The important and health giving qualities of pure milk for the family and city was a subject that engaged his attention, and as a scientist and general benefactor, several years since he set aside his churns and commenced shipping pure milk to San Francisco. In this respect, residents of Tiburon Point Tract have a double assurance that they will be supplied with absolutely pure milk under all the foregoing scientific conditions from the Eagle Dairy or others owned by Dr. Lyford.

The Eagle Dairy in a picture from Lyford's Hygeia, *a brochure published in 1895. Fences and railroad trestle are newly whitewashed. To the left of the house is a salvaged ship's cabin where Dr. Lyford experimented with embalming. Above is a page from the brochure.*

LYFORD'S HYGEIA

THE one supreme possession of man—the pearl whose price is beyond computation—without which the greatest gifts of fortune are as nothing—is health. Man, ambitious and masterful, full of energy, and ready to strive for the wealth which he sees always in the dazzling vista of the future, spends the best years of his life in piling up the riches, which, following the advice of the Roman merchant to his son, he has accumulated by methods oftimes more than doubtful, and then when he plucks the ripe fruit and places it to his lips finds it tasteless. The health, which, if properly cared for, would have enabled him to enjoy his wealth, has fled and all his millions are apparently unable to recall it.

There seems to be a combination in the elements and especially nature's provision for a bountiful supply of pure water that will enable refined men and women to establish an Elysium at Tiburon Point Tract. In connection with the number of springs of pure water that gush out near the summit of the highest hills and trickle down to the bay shore, there is a history that has given a good name and a fame that has extended to all portions of the globe as to the absolute purity of California water. For several years in the history of California the chief supply of water for sea-going vessels was taken from the great reservoir near Lyford's Glen Cove which was fed from the springs on this tract of land. The excellent quality of this water that seems to have been doubly distilled by the forces of nature in forcing it through the granite rocks at the foot of Mt. Tamalpais was recognized by seamen as the most desirable water for vessels and no superior to be found in the world. The maps of subdivisions of this tract will be in regular series and made in folios, a feature that has been highly commended by officials and searchers of records.

Of this marvelous spot, which even now events are shaping to become the most far-famed health resort the world has known, of its matchless combination of location, climate, water facilities, freedom from fogs, noxious vapors, and in a word, total immunity from all those elements which retard growth and ultimately destroy life, much has been written, but its true story and the story of the almost supernatural foresight which seems to have guided him who has been foremost in bringing its advantages, its unequaled climatic conditions before the world, is yet to be told. Dr. Benjamin F. Lyford, the retired physician, scientist and inventor, whose name is known throughout the civilized world, has searched the world over for the ideal location and climate, and here at Tiburon, with its matchless ensemble of attractions, he has found the spot where the prescience of genius was located, the fountain of youth and health. Foreseeing its future greatness, he commenced a series of experiments and scientific tests with the most delicate instruments and to him was unfolded a condition of atmospheric currents that were several degrees warmer than in the surrounding locality and rarified air by the sea-shore. Dr. Lyford prevailed on Peter Donahue, the millionaire, to pierce the mountain which shut this fair spot from the outer world, thus bringing it into direct contact with the surrounding country. This being done, he at once commenced to improve and beautify his property. Of this and its peerless environment our reader will be informed in the following article.

N Glen Cove, more properly known as Lyford's Glen, is a marvel of nature so harmonious in location and environment and so blended with scenic attractions that it has been the purpose of the owner, Dr. Lyford, to have here situated a great sanitarium or a seaside resort and watering place that shall equal any one in the world. The course followed by the steamers from San Francisco to Tiburon, keeps clear from the heavy cross currents and in this respect is the most favored route on the Bay of San Francisco. The accompanying cuts and photo-engravings give a forceful idea of the many picturesque views in this region, but cannot be hardly realized unless by personal observation.

In modern civilization, large cities and concentrated population have been created by a favored environment of climate, productive lands and ample facilities in water communication connected by a safe harbor for large ships. These adjuncts are absolutely necessary, and we may add that without any one of these the presence of the others is of no avail in creating a great, cosmopolitan center of trade, from whose wharves ships shall sail for all parts of the habitable globe. Regarding the Bay of San Francisco from this standpoint, it stands pre-eminently the peer of any, and in many respects it has no equal. The rapid growth of California has been largely due to facilities which the Bay of San Francisco affords in its vast extent and its capacity for all the ships of the world to lie at anchor.

These excerpts from Lyford's Hygeia, *a brochure from 1895 advertising the first subdivision on the Tiburon peninsula, illustrate the perfect union of style and idea — both grandiose.*

A T one time;—It is a prophecy that is being verified; that San Francisco would be the connecting link between the Orient and the Occident and become the largest and most populous city in the world. In all lands and among all people there is a concensus of opinion and a unanimity seldom seen, that draws to our State the wealth, noted personages, and the home seekers of the United States, Europe and Asia. These come under various auspices; some to add to their already great wealth; others to recoup exhausted fortunes; others for health.

The attractions of our City and Bay are not confined to commercial facilities, as the scenic beauty around the Bay whose shore line extends over two hundred miles, and a climate that seems to be the acme of perfection, due mainly to the Kuro-Siwo or Pacific Ocean current flowing along the coast, with an accompanying stream of warm air, and to the Coast and Sierra Nevada Mountain ranges. Both are equal modifiers and equalizers of temperature and rainfall. The ocean factor determines generally the direction of atmospheric motion over the State, and charges the air with moisture, raising low and depressing high temperatures. Altitude, typography and proximity to the ocean and mountains are the principal causes of variation between sections.

In all great cities the noxious gases that exude from decomposition, and *especially* during the night, foster diseases, lessen vitality, and are the primal cause of the great mortality in centers of dense population. It has become among all energetic people the universal custom to live in suburban homes adjac-nt to the metropolis of their respective place of business. There is in this system of economies a higher civilization, a more refined life, a more perfect development of the body politic, state and nation.

F OR many years Dr. Lyford has been fully alive to the matchless location of this favored spot; of its accessibility to the great metropolis with its vast population; of its balmy, invigorating atmosphere free from fogs and malaria; and with the unswerving intention of perfecting his property so as to make it an earthly Elysium, he has toiled and planned. It would be impossible to detail the seemingly insuperable obstacles which have been overcome by tenacity of purpose, but it is sufficient to say that the desire of his life is now accomplished, and before many months Tiburon Point Tract will be transformed into the most beautiful and select health resort on the Coast. Even now there are hundreds, weary with the carking cares of city life, who look forward to a residence on this spot as an epoch of their lives, and who will make it their permanent abiding place. Another important feature is that Dr. Lyford exercises great care in selecting his grantees, only those of unimpeachable character being given deeds to lots. That there will be more persons desiring to purchase than can be accommodated is evident, for the health enjoyed by the few now living there and their immunity from disease are favorably commented on.

In fact it has become a subject of general notoriety among residents in this vicinity that a large number of chronic cases of nervous diseases, pulmonary complaints and ailments common to woman have been cured by taking a residence in this locality. This knowledge of the curative and recuperative condition of the climate and ozone of the shore and bay has induced a number of persons to seek this locality as a sanitarium with its yet but meagre accommodations.

It has been the purpose of the founder of this Hygeia and an ambition as the crowning act of his life to build a city at Point Tiburon that would be a great sanitarium, the abode of a strong, healthy and happy community, and in this connection to establish a higher plane of existence and work out a very interesting social and physiological problem for mankind.

F OLLOWING these lines, all conveyances of realty will be made with restrictions that will keep out the vices and vampires common to all communities.

In presenting this work it has been the purpose to show certain portions of Tiburon Tract in all its many attractions and scenic effects in kaleidoscopic view.

It is a wonderland in its location, environment and condition for building suburban residences and making ideal homes.

The founder after years of toil and scientific investigation has a fixed and settled purpose to make this favored spot a center of education, science, art, and an abode where there should be contentment, longevity and a happy healthful life. To those who may peruse this souvenir of Lyfords's Hygeia or Goddess of Health, no conception can be had of the favored climate, topography and advantages for residence unless by an actual and personal inspection.

Readers may note a central contradiction in the ideas set forth: a man who abhors dense populations is hoping that San Francisco will be the largest city in the world.

Little Reed Dairy Ranch had flourished for more than thirty years when this picture was taken in 1905. The Manuel Borges family lived in the house in the trees at upper right. Their granddaughter, Mary Bernard, was born here, and gave this picture to the Landmarks Society. Del Mar School now occupies the site.

In 1850, just 705 pounds of butter were produced in California; by 1880 the total was fourteen million pounds, almost twenty per cent of it from Marin County, which led all others in dairying. (Courtesy Mary Silva)

The Years Between

The four decades between 1842, when John Reed died, and 1882, when Peter Donahue came to Tiburon Point, were turbulent in the history of California. Waves of immigrants poured into the state, San Francisco roared into life on the windy peninsula across the bay, fortunes were made and lost in the gold fields, a railroad crossed the continent. In Marin, the population rose to 11,320 by 1880, with dairy farms, vegetable gardens, sawmills and fisheries, and a fleet of small craft shuttling across the bay.

The pace of life and change on the Tiburon Peninsula during these forty years was slow indeed. In 1856, Hilaria Sanchez Reed Garcia, twice widowed, received confirmation of her title to Rancho Corte Madera. Her children grew up and took charge of the herds grazing free on the grasslands; John Joseph, Inez, and Hilarita all had their brands registered on July 17, 1860. Gradually the wild Mexican cattle were replaced by dairy cows, and a new industry grew. Fresh milk and butter brought premium prices in San Francisco, only a short boat ride away.

One attempt at a settlement on the Tiburon Peninsula during this period was "California City," an improbable paper metropolis dreamed up by Benjamin R. Buckelew, a brash New Yorker who arrived in California in 1846 and immediately set about getting his hands on as much real estate as he could, by fair means or foul, usually the latter. In a complex maneuver, he acquired 320 acres of Reed's rancho on the east side of the Tiburon Peninsula, where Paradise Cay is today. He then bought a shipload of unclaimed prefabricated houses, laid out a town in 1852, set up a hotel and a few houses, and sat back to wait for a flood of buyers. They never came.

Another settlement briefly took root in the same area in the 1860's. It boasted a saloon in 1864, the first on the peninsula by twenty years, and daily ferry service to San Francisco aboard the oyster sloop *John Palmer*. The settlement sputtered out as mysteriously as it had come to life.

A few small industries came to take advantage of the proximity to the bay and other resources. Brickmakers, finding clay deposits along both shores of the peninsula, set up kilns to supply the San Franciscans who had been importing bricks from the East Coast and Europe at great expense because of the urgent need for fireproof buildings. An 1869 map shows six brickyards, one belonging to Tom Boggins. One yard on the east shore, owned by one P. Lubbersmeier, supplied bricks — at $14 per thousand — for the construction of Fort Point in San Francisco.

Great codfish banks were first discovered in the north Pacific in 1863, and soon Tiburon had a new industry. Great racks of fish lay drying along the sand spits, beginning with Israel Kashow's drying yard on Beach Road. Kashow's seafaring partner, Nicholas Bichard, sent ships north to the codfish banks every year from 1870 to 1888.

Two other codfisheries, the Thomas W. McCollam Company on the west side of Belvedere, and Lynde & Hough on the east shore of the peninsula, merged in 1904 as the Union Fish Company, and continued to operate the Belvedere yard until put out of business by a fire in 1937.

These companies produced dried, flaked fish, by-products such as "Dr. Fisherman's Lotion for Men and Beasts," and thousands of gallons of Okhotsk Sea Cod Liver Oil, one of the vilest substances ever devised by man, fed to several generations of helpless babies on the sage advice of physicians.

In 1866, the Morgan Oyster Company was staking imported oysters in beds in the shallows of the bay on the west shore of Strawberry Point, along what is now San Rafael Avenue, and at the north end of Belvedere lagoon. For some reason, the spawn would not thrive in the bay, so that the oysters, brought in from Washington and from the east, could only be fattened here, not transplanted. John S. Morgan pulled up stakes (literally) in about 1876, when winter storms and flooding made the beds unprofitable.

In the 1870's, after several calamitous explosions in San Francisco powder plants, the Vigolite Powder company moved to the east shore of the Tiburon peninsula. Peter Donahue used powder from this plant to blast out three tunnels for his track from Tiburon to San Rafael, and to blow up the bluff at Point Tiburon in order to construct his yards. In 1877 the frankly named Hazard Powder Company built two large brick powder magazines and a pier on the east shore.

Surely the most spectacular industry to spring up on the Tiburon Peninsula during these years was shipwrecking.

Four milkers, still with milking stools strapped around their waists, obliged a photographer by stopping work long enough for their picture to be taken. The year was about 1900, and the place the Hilarita Dairy (also called Souza's and later Avila's) on the site now occupied by Reed School. In the background, besides the traditional well-fed dairy cats, is the wash house, which appears to be a cabin from one of the old ships which had been stripped and burned in this area. (Courtesy Mary Silva)

Outmoded, damaged, or abandoned old ships were hauled up to the spits and broken up, their valuable iron, copper, and brass fittings salvaged, their hulls burned or used for lumber. Many cabins from wrecked ships turned up on the dairy farms, to be used as milk-house, chicken coop, bunkhouse, or (at the Lyfords' ranch) as a laboratory for experiments in embalming.

In 1886 the salvage yards were moved from the west to the east shore of the peninsula. Here the greatest prize was the steamer *China*, wrecked in 1886. She yielded nearly forty tons of metal, as well as lumber and glass enough to build several shanties for workmen. The social salon became a private home on Beach Road, and is now known as the China Cabin.

The East Shore

One cove on the east shore of the Tiburon Peninsula has undergone dramatic changes in the past hundred years, and has accumulated a remarkable history, most of it nautical.

First it was the site of an Indian village, whose inhabitants may well have boarded the *San Carlos* in 1775. A brick kiln operated in the cove in the 1860's. The firm of Lynde and Hough built the first long wharf, where tall-masted sailing ships brought codfish from 1877 to 1904. In that year the site became a U.S. Navy Coaling Station, where ships took on fuel. The scale of this operation was astonishing. Coal brought by ship from eastern ports was arranged in mountainous piles by cranes running on rails. A massive concrete foundation, like a great viaduct built on arches, remains from this period, as do a large square house with a porch, and a water tank with conical roof, perched on hillsides above.

In 1931 the coaling station closed, and the California Maritime Academy moved in to begin training merchant seamen, with coal dust still blowing across the parade grounds. Two years later the John Roebling Company bought the adjacent property and began shipping in wire from eastern steel mills and twisting cables for the suspension of Golden Gate Bridge.

As the threat of war loomed, the U.S. Navy established a net depot in the cove in August, 1940. Sailors on horseback rode the perimeter to guard the depot. Thousands of men were trained here to handle nets during World War II, and miles of nets were made and maintained for Pacific Navy bases. The Hilarita housing project, built in 1942 for navy personnel, changed the look of Tiburon, over the hill. Today the town hall and police station occupy two buildings remaining from this project. (See page 31)

The McCollam Fishing & Trading Co.

The McCollam Fish Company built a plant at Pescada Landing on the west shore of Belvedere in the late 1870's, when the island was still open pastureland. For sixty years codfish from the north Pacific were dried and processed here.

By 1909, the plant, now the Union Fish Company, had changed little, but trees were covering the island.
Below: The fishery closed in 1937, and the buildings were eventually converted to artists' studios, shown here in 1963. Soon after that date these were demolished to make room for West Shore Road. One occupant said as the buildings were hauled away, "There goes the last smell." (Photo: Anna Jean Cole)

The Barkentine Fremont Arrived From Sand Point Yesterday With 167,000 Codfish Aboard. She Came In Under Full Sail and Made California City Without Taking in a Stitch of Canvas.

CAME IN WITH ALL SAIL SET.

The Fremont Made Her Way to California City Unaided.

SEEN FROM SAUSALITO.

She Made a Pretty Picture Working Her Way Through the Shipping.

The first of the fleet from Sand Point got in yesterday. She is the barkentine Fremont and has 167,000 codfish aboard. There was a fair wind and a strong wind, so instead of taking a tug Captain Bowes sailed his vessel in and worked her to California City under full canvas. As she passed Sausalito hundreds of people turned out to see her, and the crews of the British ships lying in Richardsons Bay admired her as she glided along. The vessel is consigned to the Lynde & Hough Company and the fish will be cured at California City. The catch of codfish has been a very good one this year, but the demand for the California prepared article is so great that there will be no diminution in the price.

The Fremont made the run from Sand Point in the good time of sixteen days, and Captain Bowes could not see why he should take a tug when he had a fair wind. For the first time almost in the history of the port the Fremont sailed right to her anchorage and never shortened sail until within half a mile of California City.

AN OVERDUE STORY EXPLODED.

Artists were often hired by newspapers to illustrate fast-breaking stories which did not allow time for slow procedures of photo-engraving. The artist (in this case W.A. Coulter, a famous marine painter) was rushed to the scene to make a quick sketch. At the newspaper office the drawing was engraved by hand on a metal plate for printing in that day's edition.

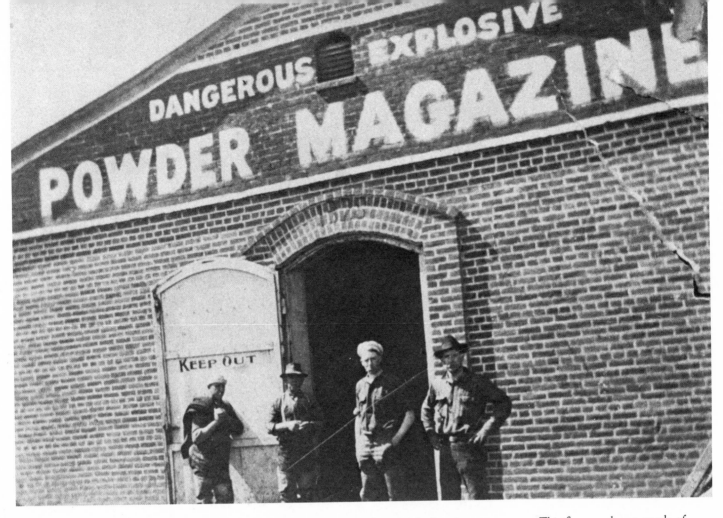

Powder companies built on the east shore of Tiburon in 1877 because the location was remote. This fine warehouse, made of Tiburon bricks, belonged to the Hazard Powder Co., near today's Seafirth. The crack at right is in the picture, not the building.

This 1899 advertisement lists a variety of useful substances for the man who wants to leave his mark on the world. With products like these, a man could level a bluff and build a railroad yard in a few months, with no concern for environmental impact.

These hardy sailors, working on a codfishing ship based in Tiburon, dangle above their tool buckets on the high seas. The picture is undated. (Courtesy Stanley Cocks)

Opposite, top: The Coaling Station (1904-1930) supplied fuel for Navy ships as America became the world's leading naval power. All that remains of the machinery is a row of concrete arches, visible (below) in front of the Tiburon Marine Laboratory, shown in 1962. Opposite, bottom: A ship unloads coils of steel wire to be twisted into cables for the Golden Gate Bridge in 1935.

*Divers from the Tiburon Marine Lab
scoop up plankton for a study of the
marine food chain.*

(Courtesy National Marine Fisheries Service)

*Scientists conduct offshore research
aboard the NOAA research vessel David
Starr Jordan.*

Four ships in Tiburon Cove await dismantling in 1886. The largest is the steam sidewheeler China, *only twenty years old, whose social salon is about to become a fixture on Beach Road. The ferries and trains have been operating for two years; the train shed is being built.* (Courtesy San Francisco Maritime Museum)

The depot's first and biggest job came before the war, when a six-thousand-ton, seven-mile net was made and stretched across the Bay from Sausalito to San Francisco. This job was almost complete by December 7, 1941. The net guarded the harbor from Japanese submarine attack, expected daily during the war.

In May, 1945, the Navy announced plans to take over the entire peninsula (3,603 acres), excepting only the railroad and downtown Tiburon, for a huge ammunition supply station to be built at Ring Point. Construction was well underway, and a good many people had moved out, their houses condemned and closed, when the Japanese surrendered and the plan was scrapped.

In 1958, the Net Depot was closed down, and three years later the Tiburon Marine Laboratory took over the site to conduct research on sea life and minerals. San Francisco State University has established an environmental studies center in one of the buildings. Excess acreage was deeded to the county, and Tiburon gained two magnificent parks. The Uplands Nature preserve, twenty-four hillside acres across Paradise Drive from the Marine Lab, is accessible only by hiking. Paradise Beach Park, where the bridge cables were wound, has eighteen acres of lawns, picnic grounds and beach, with a long fishing pier.

(From the Sausalito News, September 9, 1886)

TIBURON NOTES

The old hulks of the steamer *China* and other vessels which were lying at our harbor in care of Mighell & Buttro have been removed to George Ring's place at California City, the future dismantling grounds of the firm. This was rendered necessary because of the danger to the many vessels here now and the proximity of the buildings to the old vessels to be blown up and fired.

Peter Gardner was the purchaser of the Tiburon Hotel property, the Savage estate, which was sold here at auction last Thursday.

Work is going on quite lively now, the Donahue road putting up their fine large shed under which the trains are to pass to the ferry boat the coming winter.

Climate and weather here are naturally Sausalitish, fishing ditto. Hot as blazes just now, and rock cod biting at anything, one small boy catching one weighing seven pounds on a bent pin. Charley Rudolph of the Pioneer Boat House is as fat and happy as ever and is kept busy supplying boats to the many anglers and pleasure seekers who throng our town on Saturdays and Sundays.

The earliest picture of the new Tiburon terminal shows two woodburning locomotives with steam up. One, at center, pulls a work train; the second is at far left, where dump cars like the four at right are being loaded with rock blasted out of the bluff. Left of center is a primitive turntable.

The Ferryboat James M. Donahue is in the new slip, at left; a roofed, open shed has been built for passengers. The coaches at right do not appear to be the deluxe new ones Donahue had ready for opening day.

At bottom, a lone cow asserts her rights, and reminds us of the very necessary attachment on the front of each locomotive. These details — even the cow — suggest that this picture could have been taken as early as 1883, when the line was still under construction. (Courtesy Hap and Z Smith)

The Iron Horse Comes to Shark Point

For a long time it looked as if history might pass Shark Point by entirely. By 1880, Marin County was dotted with prosperous little towns from Sausalito to Point Reyes, but the only residents of Tiburon, besides the Kashows, Reeds, and Lyfords, were the Portuguese immigrants who worked at the dairies. There was no town at all.

The land title held by the Reed heirs and the long spur of Mount Tamalpais had retarded both settlement and private enterprise. The only industries, besides the dairies, were codfisheries, a gunpowder factory, a graveyard for obsolete ships, and a few brickyards.

Prospective settlers needed a reason — and a way — to come to Tiburon, and as yet there was neither.

Just at this time, an aging railroad magnate named Peter Donahue was looking for a place as close as possible to San Francisco for his passengers to transfer from the slow ferries to his fast broad-gauge railroad, the San Francisco and North Pacific.

When he had bought a controlling interest in his Sonoma County Railroad back in 1870, Donahue had planned to extend it south through Marin County to Sausalito and thus enjoy a railroad monopoly over the north bay. But while the Irishman had been busy in Sonoma, laying iron across the marshy Santa Rosa plain and banging together a little terminal called Donahue on Petaluma Creek, the port of Sausalito had been seized by a new narrow-gauge line just getting started, the North Pacific Coast.

By the time Donahue managed to build his railroad down to San Rafael in 1879, the clanking locomotives of the narrow gauge were already running north along the coast through Point Reyes and Tomales as far as Duncan's Mills, with a sidetrack from San Anselmo to San Rafael. The S.F. and N.P., with its tediously long ferry rides to San Quentin Point and to Donahue, was hard put to compete with it.

The only answer was Tiburon Point, which was the same distance (six miles) from the city as Sausalito. A ferry and rail terminal here would not only speed Sonoma-bound passengers north in a fraction of the old time, but would also capture the growing commuter traffic to San Rafael and a share of the lumber shipments from coastal mills.

At the same time, to keep ahead of its broad-gauge rival, the North Pacific Coast decided to eliminate a long circuitous pull over Collins Summit by dynamiting a tunnel through the Corte Madera Hill.

The race was on. It was fortunate that Peter Donahue liked a challenge, because a more difficult place than Tiburon Point to locate a train terminus could scarcely be imagined. His crews had to chisel out the hills that sloped steeply to the water's edge — literally turn a bluff into a plateau — before roundhouses and sheds could be built. Then they had to blast three tunnels through the ridges, sink trainload after trainload of ballast to fill the marsh between the Tiburon peninsula and the San Rafael ridge, and hammer down nine miles of iron over rock and bog and slope.

In 1882 a huge commotion filled the once tranquil air above the sandspit. To accomplish in months what might otherwise take years, Donahue imported a newfangled invention — an Ohio-made steam shovel that could fill a flatcar with rubble in three minutes. Fortified by rations of whiskey and pay bonuses, his Irish gangs also operated three steam drills around the clock, sank the piles for a ferry slip modelled on the latest New York Harbor design, built shops, a roundhouse, offices, a boarding house, depot, and a 300-foot dock.

From the wharf came a steady hammering as a brand new steamer, the *Tiburon*, slowly took shape. A long shed on the point sheltered six gleaming new passenger cars bought in New York for $30,000.

By Nov. 29, 1883, the Marin County *Journal* reported, "... this Point has made one grand advance. Its grand waterfront has a fine ferry slip, a long wharf, a railroad track, depot, machine shops, store, boarding houses, etc., part of which are already built, and all will be by spring ..."

Donahue poked through the last of his tunnels on March

Peter Donahue, the bold and brilliant engineer who built the San Francisco & North Pacific Railroad, had already introduced gas lights to San Francisco and built an entire town at his railhead in Sonoma County before he came to Tiburon.

10, 1884. The narrow gauge finished six days later, but was the first to send a train down its new route. The rivalry between them was fated to last well into the next century, with each line having its fiercely loyal supporters.

The competition had been eagerly followed by prospective railroad customers in San Rafael, then a village of 2,500 people, with unpaved streets and plank sidewalks. On April 27, the new San Francisco & San Rafael Railroad was complete, and the trains and ferries were ready to run. The Marin County *Journal* maintained strict impartiality, commenting, "The Donahue is an entirely new line and great interest is felt all around to try it. But this is partially offset by the new route of the N.P.C., which all are equally curious to ride over."

On May 1, 1884, Peter Donahue brought a load of city guests and dignitaries to Tiburon on the steamer *James M. Donahue,* and loaded them aboard the glistening new coaches for an inaugural ride. As the train steamed over the 800-foot redwood trestle and in and out of the tunnels toward the "grand and ornate" new depot at San Rafael, Donahue's guests, some of them probably already quite tipsy enough, washed down the Irishman's sandwiches with his whiskey and champagne.

The two lines announced the same price — 50 cents a round trip — and strove to outdo each other in making the best possible time. (That first trip was clocked at 50 minutes from San Francisco to San Rafael.) The new 240-foot steamer *Tiburon,* commanded by Captain Howard White, and the NPC's speedy steamer *San Rafael,* continued the rivalry by racing each other from the San Francisco wharf across the choppy waters of the bay to their respective landings.

George Harlan, in his book *Of Walking Beams and Paddle Wheels* (1951) described this high-spirited competition:

The vessels were somewhat of a match for speed, a very slight edge going to the *San Rafael.* For part of the journey, the rivals could not even see each other, but as the *San Rafael* left the slip in Sausalito, the *Tiburon* would be sighted nosing around the point of Belvedere Island, black smoke pouring from her "jam-factory" smokestack in an air of defiant challenge. Captain White often resorted to "tactical maneuvers" to gain an advantage in the race, some of these antics dangerously approaching the point of turning steamboat inspectors' hair a pure white, all the while they tried to assure themselves that the rivals were not really racing at all. The engineers joined in the spirit of the occasion by giving the piston a little prodding with the hand bar, and there were crossings made on the bay whose logs showed no time wasted on the trip.

The owner of the NPC warned his captains ominously that they would be fined five demerits if caught racing, and ten if they were caught losing to the Donahue ferry line.

Peter Donahue did not live to see the success of the San Francisco & San Rafael line — he died of pneumonia in November, 1885, nine days after inspecting the Tiburon terminal on a blustery cold day.

Throughout 1884 and 1885 preparations had been afoot not only to abandon the Donahue terminal on the Petaluma Creek altogether, but to bring those buildings that could be salvaged down by barge and flatcar to Tiburon.

The buildings that left Donahue on the flood tide in September, 1887, included shops, an engine house, and the forty-room Sonoma House hotel. So exactly was the little town of Donahue duplicated on Tiburon Point that historians must look closely at old photographs to see which town is actually shown.

At first, redwood lumber and other freight shipped through Tiburon had to be unloaded on the dock and reloaded aboard the ferries. This inconvenience was remedied in 1890 with the construction at Tiburon of the steamer *Ukiah,* which could carry sixteen railroad cars on its broad deck. Railroad workers built tracks across a new wharf and slip so that the cars could be shunted right onto the boat.

In 1890, desiring to increase business on its passenger ferries, the S.F. & N.P. built El Campo, a picnic resort three and a half miles east of Tiburon. It was the only pleasure ground on the coast reachable by steamer and on Sundays the holiday throng would line the decks to capacity. It is said that the mate, after casting off in San Francisco, would spend the crossing fighting his way through the crowds to the foredeck, emerging just in time to make the landing line fast at El Campo.

TIBURON.

There is no spot in the neighborhood of San Francisco for which Nature has done more than the stretch of country in Sausalito township commonly known as Tiburon. Up to a very recent date, man was content to let Nature do it all. It was even worse than that for it looked very much as though man was doing his best to deface and deform what was originally beautiful. About the only monument of humanity's occupation was a morgue for Uncle Sam's condemned cruisers, which were broken up and burned in the secluded haven and constituted an eyesore in the shape of rubbish and general desolation calculated to make a happy man sad. This, and a loud smelling codfish drying establishment were the only evidence of man's civilizing influence around Tiburon, up to a recent date.

About three years ago, however, old Peter Donahue, who by the way has done more for the development of this coast than any other one man, looked on the harbor of Tiburon and saw that it was good. In the dim future he realized that it must become the shipping point for a great commerce; that it must be the connecting link between the great northern trade and the metropolis of the Pacific that on the ruins of the ship ceme-

Above, an article from the Sausalito News, 1885. Below, a very early photo, possibly 1883, shows a single track over a low trestle crossing the lagoon. The bluff has been eaten away to provide fill for the terminal. On Main Street we see the back of the Tiburon Hotel, and at far right a cottage nudges Corinthian island.

(Courtesy California State Library)

A delightful, crisp panorama from about 1890 shows many new features in the railroad yards: the roundhouse at the water's edge, shops, a new pier with towers for raising the loading ramp, and a pile driver at work on the new slip for the Ukiah.

tery and codfish emporium would rise warehouses, factories and the substantial requirements of a great commerce. And Uncle Peter, who has a fondness for good things, determined to occupy this field himself. Accordingly, he extended his already constructed line from San Rafael to deep water on the sheltered shore of Point Tiburon.

The result has been a good illustration of the desolating effect of railraod enterprise, of which so much is said and sung and written. From the sleepiest and most primitive of settlements, Tiburon has suddenly been transformed into a lively, bustling, business like little place with the promise of much ahead. Already it has several lodging houses and other places of business. It is frequented daily by scores of visitors who come over the swift and splendidly equipped ferry to revel in the fair scenery, balmy air and unsurpassed fishing that Tiburon affords. Col. Donahue em-

Four matched rooming houses and the imposing Sonoma House Hotel have been floated down from Donahue Landing in Sonoma. Belvedere and Corinthian are bare except for the Corinthian Yacht Club (1886) and buildings along Beach Road. Several arks float in the lagoon.

ploys a small army of mechanics at his works. After building a commodious ferry depot and slip, he still needed considerable level ground for improvements around the terminus. As nature had failed to provide it, Col. Donahue determined to make it for himself and to this end has gone to work to tear down a small sized mountain. He is succeeding at it, as he does at everything else.

Dr. B. F. Lyford, the principal, in fact, only land owner around the terminus, has divided a large tract into lots and blocks and villa sites. These are soon to be placed on the market and will undoubtedly command a ready sale, The property combines every attraction. It is located on the borders of the bay, yet so shut in by the mainland and Angel and Kashaw's islands that it is freed from the fierce winds that vex other portions of the bay. It is diversified and picturesque. It is God's own sanitarium. It is within thirty minutes ride by ferry

In a picture taken some months later than the panorama on the preceding page, we see the progress on the new ferry slip, where the pile driver is still at work. The Pioneer Boat House in the foreground has added a front porch. In the background is the long train shed built to shelter passengers from winter rains. The James M. Donahue *is in the slip. A gate separates Main Street from the railroad yards.*

from San Francisco. Last, but not least, the land is held at the lowest figures. All Tiburon wants to make it one of the ambitious suburbs of San Francisco is a little pushing.

In the near future, Tiburon has the practical assurance of a great accession. It will be the location for the shops of the San Francisco and North Pacific Railroad and this will bring to it an increase of population of several hundred.

Should the railroad be extended up the Coast to and beyond the Oregon line, the location of the shops here alone would make Tiburon a place of importance. But, as has been shown above, the locality has intrinsic merits that must be appreciated as soon as known. Tiburon has a future before it that will not long remain unfulfilled.

The NEWS will particularize concerning Tiburon, its inhabitants, etc., more fully in later issues.

At the San Francisco end of the ferry boat run was this handsome building at the foot of Market Street, which had several massive ferry slips behind it. The sign in the gable says "S.F. & N.P.R.R. San Rafael & Tiburon Ferry." Buggies, wagons, and horse-drawn streetcars wait in front. Note the charming little two-story building at left, no more than 12 X 20 feet, yet beautifully trimmed and symmetrical, looking rather surprised. (Courtesy Bancroft Library)

Daniel Boehm

Steamer
Tiburon

FIRST-CLASS
MEALS

MODERATE
PRICES

Restaurant

Top: The San Rafael Local is ready to leave the Tiburon depot
(now called the Donahue Building) in the 1890's.
Bottom: Passengers hurry from the San Rafael train to the waiting ferry, circa 1903. (Courtesy Bancroft Library)

Sweeney
Wm Babcock

The James M. Donahue, *named for Peter Donahue's son, was the first ferry to serve Tiburon. Built in 1875, she was 208 feet* *long and could carry 500 passengers. Luxurious appointments included red plush seats, a grand staircase, and a dining salon.* *Retired in 1921, she spent her last days moored at San Quentin as a shrimp fishery.* (Courtesy Bancroft Library)

(Roy Graves Collection)

By the late 1890's Belvedere has acquired many fine houses. Main Street's north side is filling up, and the railroad yards are neat as a pin. *(Roy Graves Collection)*

Hilarita Station, near today's Reed School, was a flag stop for passengers or freight.

Three miles from the Tiburon Depot was Reed Station, serving the John Joseph Reeds and their neighbors. It boasted a station-master and a waiting room with window. Mail addressed "Reed's Station, Marin County, Cal." was delivered here promptly. The station stood between today's Karen Way and Corte San Fernando, a quarter-mile from Blackfield Drive.

SAN FRANCISCO AND NORTH PACIFIC RAILROAD.
GENERAL OFFICE, 430 MONTGOMERY ST., SAN FRANCISCO, CAL.

PETER DONAHUE, President.	ARTHUR HUGHES, General Manager.
JAMES M. DONAHUE, Vice-President.	PETER J. McGLYNN, G. P. & T. A.
THOMAS I. BERGIN, Treasurer.	CHAS. THORN, JR., Gen. Freight Agent.
THOS. W. JOHNSTON, Secretary and Auditor.	H. C. WHITING, Supt., San Rafael.

FROM SAN FRANCISCO.					April 5, 1885. A—Daily, except Sundays. B—Sundays only.	TO SAN FRANCISCO.				
Pass. B		Pass A	Pass A	Miles from S. F.		Pass. A	Pass. A	Pass. A	Pass. B	Pass B
a. m.		p. m.	a. m.			a. m.	p. m.			p. m.
8 00		3 30	7 45	0	Lv. San Francisco Ar.	8 50	6 05			6 10
8 35		4 05	8 20	6	Tiburon	8 20	5 30			5 30
8 38		4 08	8 23	7½	Hilarita	8 16	5 25			5 26
8 44		4 14	8 29	9½	Reeds	8 11	5 22			5 21
8 51		4 21	8 36	12½	Green Brae	8 05	5 11			5 10
8 54		4 24	8 39	14	S. Q. & S. R. Crossing	8 02	5 08			5 06
9 00		4 30	8 45	15	San Rafael	8 00	5 05			5 00
9 16		4 50	9 00	20	Millers	7 40	4 50			4 42
9 24		4 56	9 07	23	Pacheco	7 33	4 42			4 34
9 32		5 03	9 15	26	Novato	7 25	4 34			4 26
9 40		5 09	9 25	29	Burdells	7 18	4 27			4 17
9 55		5 22	9 36	35½	Junction	7 04	4 13			4 03
10 00		5 25	9 40	36½	Petaluma	7 00	4 10			4 00
10 08		5 35	9 48	39½	Elys	6 48	4 01			3 51
10 10		5 38	9 50	40½	Penns Grove	6 44	3 59			3 49
10 12		5 40	9 52	41	Goodwins	6 42	3 57			3 47
10 17		5 46	9 57	43½	Pages	6 37	3 52			3 42
10 22		5 51	10 02	46	Cotate	6 32	3 47			3 37
10 27		5 56	10 07	48½	Oak Grove	6 28	3 42			3 32
10 35		6 05	10 15	51½	Santa Rosa	6 20	3 35			3 25
10 45		6 15	10 25	56	Fulton	6 10	3 22			3 12
10 53		6 23	10 33	57½	Mark West	6 02	3 15			3 05
11 00		6 30	10 40	60½	Windsor	5 55	3 07			2 57
11 10		6 39	10 49	64½	Grants	5 45	2 57			2 47
11 15		6 45	10 55	66½	Healdsburg	5 40	2 52			2 42
11 25		6 54	11 04	70½	Littons	5 31	2 42			2 32
11 35		7 03	11 13	74½	Clairville	5 22	2 32			2 22
11 49		7 16	11 26	80½	Asti	5 09	2 19			2 09
12 00		7 25	11 35	84½	Cloverdale	5 00	2 10			2 00

a. m.			a. m.				p. m.			p. m.
10 45			10 25	56	Fulton		3 22			3 10
10 51			10 30	58	Meachams		3 10			3 04
10 57			10 36	60	Carrigers		3 00			2 58
11 03			10 42	62	Laguna		2 50			2 52
11 09			10 50	64	Forestville		2 40			2 48
11 15			11 00	66	Green Valley		2 30			2 40
11 25			11 20	69	Korbels		2 05			2 30
11 35			11 40	72	Ar. Guerneville Lv.		1 45			2 20

BETWEEN SAN FRANCISCO AND SAN RAFAEL.

This timetable for the San Francisco - Cloverdale run is from the 1880's.

With a cloud of smoke and the hiss of steam, a passenger train pulls out of the long train shed around 1895. Spare fuel is stacked on the flatcar at left. The leading passenger car on this train, just behind the freight car, is now a private home on Tiburon Boulevard.

(Roy Graves Collection)

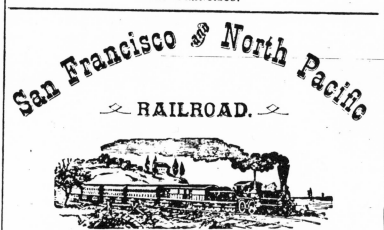
This advertisement from the 1880's announces convenient connections with stagecoach lines in the north.

The early issues of the Sausalito News carried items from Tiburon in every edition.

An Artesian well 2,000 feet deep is to be bored at Point Tiburon by the S. F. & N. P. R. R. Co. The Standard Well Boring Company has the contract and begun work with a four inch drill. It will be near the round-house on made grounds.

Opposite: Sleek and polished, Engine No. 10 poses in Tiburon, April 5, 1903. with a neat stack of wood in the tender. The bulbous smokestack is a spark arrester. This woodburner was scrapped in 1937, after 54 years of service.

Three mechanics and a friend rest from their work on a flatcar in the early 1900's.

Top: A railroad section hand prepares to leave in his gasoline motor car for a job down the line. (Preston H. Kane Collection)

Above: Engine No. 14, built in 1888, was named Tiburon. In the center, back of the bell, was the sand dome, which dispensed sand to keep wheels from slipping on grades. The picture is dated 1903.

Opposite: The Tiburon, built here in 1884, served for nearly forty years. She was used as a dormitory and mess hall for strikebreakers during the big railroad strike of 1922, then was dismantled and sold for scrap. In the early 1900's (top) she began to carry a new kind of cargo: the horseless carriage. The happy trio have found a rope in case of brake failure.

(Roy Graves Collection)

A DAY AT EL CAMPO.

It Is a Pretty Place for Picnicking and Camping.

Three Hundred Visitors on the First Trip—A Place Where Hoodlums Cease From Troubling and the Weary Are at Rest.

Just three miles east of Tiburon, on the mainland of Marin, is a pleasant little nook embayed from the aggressive cold winds and fogs; a place abounding in cunning nooks, bosky glens and cool verdurous

from the new picnic grounds at El Campo, and one mile from the old ship-breaking yard at California City.

The railroad company has provided a nicely graded road on the side of the cliff, between the steamer landing and the pavilion on the picnic grounds, so that not only is a landing easy and possible at all stages of the tide, but the most infirm or aged patron of the road can reach the grounds without difficulty or unnecessary exertion.

There is facility for camping, bathing, boating or fishing, a mild air, warm water and absolute freedom from the incursions of hoodlums. Foreseeing a possible invasion of this future family resort by the hoodlum element the railroad company has secured the services of two Marin County officers and an assurance from the authorities at San Rafael that all hoodlums coming within their purview will be dealt with according to their deserts. It is a special feature of the El Campo grounds that they are not accessible by road or rail, so that the company can easily confine the patronage to decent people. The picnic grounds cover 100 acres, beautifully shaded and with

EL CAMPO AND DOME HILL.

shade; a spot hereafter to be known to the respectable section of the picnic community as El Campo. The San Francisco and North Pacific Railroad formally inaugurated the opening of the picnic grounds yesterday by a water party on the steamer Ukiah.

Invitations had been sent to about 500 persons and 300 responded. Among those who accepted the company's hospitality were: Judge Garvey of Ukiah, Luman Wadham, Carlton C. Crane, J. F. McCarty, Samuel Miller, Jesse Mehan, Amos Burr, Colonel F. S. Chadbourne, W. D. Sanborn, Colonel Edwards, W. F. K. Zook, Russell J. Wilson, Henry T. Scott, Gordon E. Sloss, George Bower, Martin Corcoran and about 100 representatives of the railroad interests. There were fully 100 ladies in the party, and to enliven matters en route Blum's Band was taken along.

The Ukiah left the wharf at 1 o'clock in the afternoon and took the route skirting Angel Island on the east side, so as to avoid the tide-rip through Raccoon Straits. The weather was perfection, and the afternoon breeze was not only sharp enough to dispel the summer heat, but sufficiently pronounced to drive the more delicate members of the expedition under cover. Once under the lee of Angel Island and the air became soft and balmy, a condition of affairs which was universally commented on when the party left the steamer at the new landing stage, a couple of hundred yards

a canyon at the west end, through which runs a spring of pure water.

The company's main idea is to provide a spot at which families unable to afford the expense of a long journey out of town may find accommodations for camping out by the day or week or month with the advantage of journeying to and from town twice or thrice daily at a nominal fee.

Soon after the arrival of the party yesterday Blum's Band struck up a waltz, and soon a number of couples were testing the spacious pavilion floor. Then an adjournment was had to the picnic-grounds, where lunch-tables had been spread under the trees, and the guests sat down to a cold collation. Under this exhilarating influence acquaintance and mutual esteem ripened early, and gentlemen hitherto distinguished for diffidence and excessive modesty were moved to speak a few words in praise of the surroundings and the enterprise of the railroad company. Among the speakers were: Judge Garvey, Colonel Nelson and Carlton C. Crane, on behalf of the visitors; Messrs. Burgin and H. C. Whiting for the company, and E. F. Moran for the press. The party then roamed up the canyon, inspected the beauties of Dome Hill and the many romantic spots along the beach, and the old, old resorts of the Marin County Indians, returning in time to indulge in a few dances in the pavilion and then departing on the Ukiah at 5 o'clock. Colonel Menton had entire charge of the trip.

The Ukiah will make trips daily hereafter to El Campo, at hours which will be announced in THE CALL.

El Campo, a picnic resort opened on the east shore of the peninsula by the San Francisco & North Pacific Railroad in 1891, was enormously popular for many years. During this period gangs of ruffians from the city would go on Sunday excursions in Marin, often ruining the enjoyment of their fellow passengers by drinking and fighting. Elaborate precautions were taken at El Campo, explains the article at left, from the San Francisco Call, July, 1891.

Opposite, top: The Society of California Pioneers enjoyed an outing at El Campo in September, 1898. The ladies daringly lift their skirts for wading; a more conservative gentleman rows a boat in a top hat. The ferryboat Ukiah, to the right of the boathouse, provided transportation.

Opposite, bottom: Employees of W. & J. Sloane Furniture Company in San Francisco gather for a panoramic portrait (this is only the right one-third of the whole photograph) at El Campo in 1925.

"We're Going to El Campo"

A TRIP ON THE

San Francisco and North Pacific Ry.

Through Marin and Sonoma Counties,
and the famed Russian River and Ukiah
Valleys, reveals the grandest scenery of
the Golden State. For health, pleasure
and recreation, this, the

PICTURESQUE ROUTE

is without a rival

For detailed information, apply at 650 Market St. (Chronicle
Bldg.) or General Office, Cor. Sansome and
California Streets

H. C. WHITING,
General Manager

R. X. RYAN,
General Passenger Agent

The three young ladies in the advertisement above (1896) seem to be sharing a very private joke. (Courtesy Bancroft Library)

This map of the S.F. & N.P. route was published in the 1892 annual report. (Courtesy Keith Morrison)

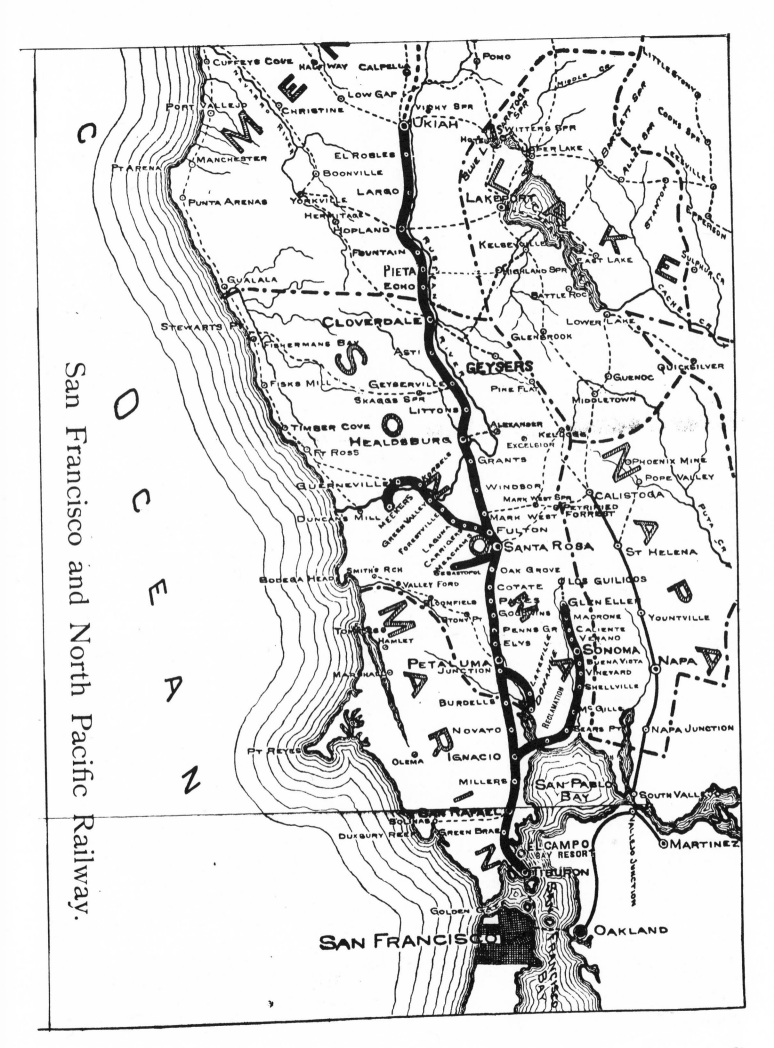

San Francisco and North Pacific Railway.

51

THIRD · ANNUAL · REPORT
— OF THE —
SanFrancisco
AND
NorthPacific
Railway

JUNE 30th,
←1892→

TIBURON

The S.F. & N.P. went public in 1890, and began issuing annual reports to stockholders. Written in a very personal tone and decorated with charming artwork, these reports are full of detailed information about Tiburon, as the excerpts opposite show.

Below: The magnificent ferry Ukiah, built in the Tiburon yards and launched in January, 1891, could carry four thousand passengers and sixteen loaded freight cars. At 291 feet long and 78 feet wide, she was the largest ferryboat in the world. During World War I the Ukiah saw such heavy service that she was rebuilt in 1923, emerging as the Eureka (bottom, opposite). The Eureka made her last Marin run in February, 1941, and was then transferred to the Oakland route. The huge walking-beam paddle-wheeler is now on display at the Hyde Street Pier in San Francisco, a part of the National Maritime Museum.

(Roy Graves Collection)

New sand house, Tiburon................		
New ferry slip, Tiburon................		
Cost of constructing apron and hoisting gear as per contract..	$6,950 00	
Raising, filling and grading approach, constructing bulkhead, dredging, piling, driving, capping and painting, rails and laying, etc.................	14,540 12	
El Campo picnic grounds.............		
Clearing and prepar'g grounds,	$2,335 15	
Constructing dock........ ...	1,751 22	
Building pavilion, tables, galleries, fencing, merry-goround, etc................	5,708 35	
Real Estate (purchase of tide lot)................	700 00	
Sundries...................	704 07	
	$11,198 79	

Steamer Ukiah.—The crown sheets were renewed in all the furnaces, and extra stay bolts put in back connection of boiler in order to strengthen same. Ends of steamer changed to fit the slip built by the Harbor Commissioners, and the upper deck strengthened.

Steamer Tiburon.—Boiler and engine thoroughly repaired. Ten new arms put in the wheels. Ends of main deck over rudder renewed. New sheathing on deck. Bottom cleaned and copper patched while on dry dock. All the hull and portion of joiner works painted, cabin carpeted, and all parts of the steamer put in first-class condition.

Steamer James M. Donahue.—Extensive repairs on engine, boiler, hull and cabin. Bottom cleaned and copper patched while on the dry dock, and the entire steamer newly painted and carpeted throughout.

TRANSFERRING FREIGHT.

On October 19th, 1891, an important change was made in the manner of transferring freight between your terminus at Tiburon and San Francisco, on the opposite side of the bay. Previous to that date all freight was taken across the bay loose on board steamers and schooners; but with the building of the car transfer steamer "Ukiah" and a new ferry slip at Tiburon by your company, and the construction of a ferry slip, belt railroad and freight sheds by the State on the water front in San Francisco, we were enabled to transport loaded cars from all points on our line to San Francisco, and vice versa, without breaking bulk. This arrangement has given great satisfaction to our shippers, and has relieved your company of heavy expenses for lost and damaged freight necessarily incident to handling freight three times while in transit. The charges ($900 a month) made by the State through its Harbor Commissioners for the use of slip, tracks, ground, freight sheds, etc., necessary to handle your freight business in San Francisco, we believe to be excessive, and hope to have them reduced after we are able to show, from the first year's business, that the amount of freight transported does not justify such terminal charges.

(*Roy Graves Collection*)

Boilermakers at the Northwestern Pacific shops in Tiburon literally made boilers for the steam locomotives, and maintained and repaired the steam tubes, among other chores. The men in this 1905 picture are (left to right) Byrne, Kerona, Beggs, Hooper, Bradley, Creighton, and Grbac. (Courtesy of Mrs. Matt Grbac)

This list of salaries from the 1892 annual report shows that the master mechanic was by far the best paid employee — and with good reason. His responsibilities were enormous; his talent and experience kept the whole system running.

REPORT OF PERSONS EMPLOYED AND AMOUNT PAID
For Years ending June 30, 1891 and 1892.

OCCUPATION.	Year ending June 30, 1891		Year ending June 30, 1892	
	NO. MEN	AMOUNT.	NO. MEN	AMOUNT.
CONDUCTING TRANSPORTATION.				
Agents and clerks.....................	34	$24,923 30	34	$26,206 60
Dispatchers and operators.............	1	1,020 00	1	1,020 00
Advertising and soliciting agents.......	2	2,510 00	2	2,880 00
Conductors........................	10	11,419 00	10	11,465 15
Brakemen and baggagemen...........	14	10,471 15	14	10,664 60
Laborers...........................	8	5,265 30	9	6,527 05
Watchmen..........................	1	730 00	1	764 00
Superintendence....................	1	3,000 90	1	3,600 00
Mail carriers......................	4	422 25	4	411 00
Wood sawing gang..................	6	3,293 50	5	2,702 70
STEAMERS:				
Captains...........................	2	3,600 00	3	4,054 60
Engineers.........................	3	5,400 00	3	5,600 00
Crew..............................	32	25,355 89	31	23,932 55
	118	$97,410 39	118	$99,828 25
MOTIVE POWER AND MAINTENANCE OF CARS.				
Engineers.........................	12	$13,446 35	12	14,276 00
Firemen...........................	12	7,631 55	12	7,517 36
Hostlers and wipers.................	6	3,357 75	6	3,278 95
Foremen...........................	3	3,408 90	3	3,473 00
Machinists and helpers..............	9	6,960 70	9	7,335 15
Carpenters, car repairers and helpers....	11	9,363 75	12	9,984 25
Painters and helpers................	6	5,175 55	6	5,084 75
Blacksmiths and helpers.............	4	3,627 90	4	3,414 45
Other mechanics....................	7	5,613 85	6	5,357 70
Watchmen..........................	1	730 00	1	730 00
Laborers..........................	6	3,441 00	8	4,576 60
Master Mechanic...................	1	1,999 94	1	2,266 64
	78	$64,757 24	80	$67,294 85

STATEMENT OF NUMBER OF PASSENGERS FROM STATIONS, AND REVENUE THEREFROM.

AGENCIES.	For Year ending June 30, 1891.		For Year ending June 30, 1892.	
	Number of Passengers.	Revenue.	Number of Passengers.	Revenue.
San Francisco..........	416,141	$195,990 67	526,100	$211,9 7 26
Tiburon.................	25,312	3,350 95	34,559	4,316 55
San Rafael.............	99,170	17,154 60	85,786	14,695 15
Ignacio......	1,325	604 55	1,653	693 75
Novata................	3,833	2,003 90	4,457	2 296 60
Petaluma	36,052	28,895 30	36,117	28,648 30
Santa Rosa	42,689	42,753 45	39,809	40,792 65
Fulton.................	3,020	2,215 70	2,682	1,877 80
Windsor...............	2,342	2,281 80	2,231	2,189 35
Healdsburg............	13,311	15,767 40	12,428	15,848 15
Littons................	637	626 75	238	242 00
Geyserville	3,243	3,259 65	3,430	2,969 35
Cloverdale.............	7,013	11,205 25	5,993	9,387 05
Pieta............			59	99 15
Hopland................	3,208	4,844 60	2,802	4,229 45
Ukiah	10,847	26,818 95	8,182	25,305 10
Guerneville..	4,670	5,701 35	4,694	5,975 50
Sonoma	4,388	3,741 80	4,687	3,721 40
Glen Ellen.............	2,095	1,532 15	2,401	1,796 30
Sebastopol....	7,185	4,415 15	7,480	4,692 80
Conductors	36,106	18,947 50	43,191	21,572 90
Excursions, stage lines, etc.	81,561	24,367 44	92,378	29,803 02
Totals..............	804,148	$416,479 01	921,357	$433,089 58

MACHINERY—CAR AND STEAMER DEPARTMENT.

Total mileage of Engines during the year.................. 387,973
Mileage of Steamers.......... 47,153
Mileage of Freight Cars................... 1,691,024
Mileage of Passenger Cars............. 920,632

The Equipment available for service at the close of the year was as follows:

Locomotives	17	Section Road Cars............	8
Passenger Cars............	41	Push Cars	28
Excursion Cars............	7	Velocipede Cars.............	2
Baggage, Mail and Express.	4	Pile-drivers' Cars	1
Box Cars...................	103	Land Pile-drivers	2
Open Stock Cars..........	13	Passenger and Freight Steam-	
Flat Cars	273	ers	8
Caboose Cars..............	2	Floating Pile-drivers.........	1
Directors' Cars	1	Steam Shovels	1
Section Hand Cars..........	33	Transfer Cars..............	1
Dump Cars...:.............	13		

There are also 24 new Box Cars now being constructed.

ENGINES.

Two Engines have been thoroughly repaired.
Three Engines have had ordinary repairs.
Three Engines painted and varnished.
Two Engines varnished.

At your pleasure resort, El Campo, there has been constructed, in addition to the wharf and pavilion, a bowling alley, shooting gallery, restaurant, merry-go-round and a great number of tables and seats, thus making it a most desirable resort for week-day picnics and pleasure seekers. The passenger business has been, and will continue to be greatly augmented by the large and increasing travel to this resort.

In Belvedere, adjoining Tiburon, there has been built, in addition to the twenty houses already erected, as stated in our last report, twenty-five more residences, and an additional number will be constructed in the near future. A growing demand exists for homes on this peninsula and it will continue to increase in popularity and population.

The property of Benjamin F. Lyford, M. D. otherwise known as "Rancho Corte Madera del Presidio" immediately adjoining the company's property on the easterly side of Tiburon, has just been placed upon the market, to be cut up and sold in building lots, in a similar manner to Belvedere peninsula. This property embraces some 4,000 acres, and has never been a source of revenue to your company. It is anticipated that there will be great demand for building lots in this locality in the immediate future; and already fifteen houses have been contracted for The climate is unsurpassed, and for a distance of several miles the water front is on San Francisco Bay. Being immediately adjacent to your Tiburon ferry landing, and only thirty minutes ferryage from San Francisco, it is a most desirable and healthful abode for business men of San Francisco and their families.

These excerpts from the 1892 annual report reflect the optimism of the growing company. (Courtesy Keith Morrison)

Carl Fennema (second row, with a black armband) worked in the office at NWP and liked to visit the other departments. He was visiting the machine shop in 1910 when a photographer stopped in. Mr. Fennema has identified most of the men: (top row) Charles McNeill, Tamburini, Canziani, Simmontachi; (second row) Walter B. McLean, Fennema, (?), Robert Salkeld, later master mechanic, Walter Royal, Masterson, Charles Heebner, Jim Murray; (third row) Charles Fryer, with hands crossed; (fourth row) Bucknum, Chester Zimmerman, John Burns; (bottom row) Lloyd Wosser, Charles O'Connell.

In giving the picture to the Landmarks Society in 1970, Carl Fennema recalled:

McNeill, Zimmerman, Burns, Wosser, O'Connell — all machinist apprentices. "Punks," they were known as. Pay: 10¢ per hour with a 2½¢ raise every six months during the four-year apprenticeship, before they could be classed as journeymen. Ten-hour day and six-day week. At Adams' barbershop a shave was 15¢ and a haircut was 25¢. A loaf of bread cost 5¢.

Opposite, above: A big engine steams along the bay near Hilarita in 1908. Below, in a picture taken from the same spot in 1984, we see strollers, cyclists, joggers on the path which replaced the railroad bed.

Locomotive No. 18 was ready to head north from the train shed in 1909. A year later this engine was destroyed in a head-on crash at Ignacio.

A Merger and a New Name

In 1907 Donahue's San Francisco & North Pacific Railroad merged with the North Shore Railroad and other lines to become the Northwestern Pacific Railroad. Two years later, passenger service to the Tiburon landing was discontinued, and it became exclusively a freight terminal and the location of the main shop, just as important but less glamorous. The only way to get to Marin County by ferry was once again by going to Sausalito. Tiburon-bound passengers had to transfer to the tiny 97-foot steamer *Requa*, (later rebuilt after a fire and rechristened the *Marin*) which stopped at the tip of Belvedere Island as well. Buses replaced the *Marin* in 1933.

In 1934 the Northwestern Pacific track through Tiburon, by then used only for freight shipments, was briefly in the limelight once again. That was the year Al Capone, former Public Enemy #1, and 52 other convicted felons were handcuffed to their seats in a barred and armored railroad car and sent off from Atlanta Penitentiary to be the first inmates at a new escape-proof Federal prison — Alcatraz.

The special train went first to Napa Junction, then "as a

surprise move in the secrecy with which the Government sought to cloak every movement in the transfer of the prisoners," reported the *San Francisco Chronicle* breathlessly on Aug. 23 "the train was shuttled on to the abandoned Tiburon line which had not been used [for passengers] in 26 years."

With the convicts still chained to their seats, the cell car and a guard car were rolled aboard a barge and floated to Alcatraz. When the last of the men were locked in their cells, Warden James A. Johnston wired the Attorney General: "FIFTY THREE CRATES FURNITURE FROM ATLANTA RECEIVED IN GOOD CONDITION, INSTALLED, NO BREAKAGE."

When the Golden Gate Bridge opened in 1937, the ferries heard their death knell in the rumbling from the automobiles and trucks crossing the bay above them. On March 1, 1941, the Sausalito-San Francisco ferries were discontinued. Passenger traffic on NWP's mainline trains declined to one train a day, then one three times a week, then, by 1958, none at all.

On June 30, 1913, NWP locomotive No. 112 crashed through a wharf into fifty feet of water.

Preston Kane, retired NWP master car repairman, took special pride in his work on No. 112, which was fished out of the bay and returned to duty. It is currently on display at the Railroad Museum in Old Sacramento, and is the only NWP locomotive still in existence.

(Preston Kane Collection)

Northwestern Pacific Locomotive No. 134, decked out in flags and bunting, stopped in the Tiburon railroad yards on its tour to promote the sale of Liberty Bonds in April, 1919. (Courtesy Carl Fennema)

Opposite: Above the Victory Train are the first Tiburon school and two early houses on Mar West.

(Courtesy Dick Williamson)

The 97-foot shuttle ferry Marin *ran to Sausalito from Tiburon with a stop at Belvedere. She was built in 1912 on the hull of the first shuttle boat, the* Requa, *which burned to the waterline. Shuttle ferries operated from 1909 until buses took over in 1933.*

This panorama gives a sweeping view of the railroad yards from the depot to Main Street in the early 1920's, showing the depot, the pedestrian walkway which enabled hill residents to cross from Main Street to Mar West, the roundhouse, the "new" shop with a full supply of spare wheels in front, and the Corinthian Yacht Club at far right. (H.C. Tibbetts, photographer; courtesy D.S. Richter).

62

This fine panorama, from the ferry slips on the left to the old lagoon on the right, shows the railroad yards at a peak of activity. At the dock are the ferryboats San Pablo, on loan to NWP from the Santa Fe, and the James M. Donahue without a stack; she had just been retired.

"Noise, Oil, Welding, and Hammering"

Until 1967, freight trains still rolled in and out of the Tiburon yards, some for maintenance, some to transfer their heavy-laden flatcars to barges for the trip across the water. Tiburon was where the big locomotives and freight cars were maintained and sometimes built or re-built. More than 2,000 cars were handled each month. A reporter in 1950 described Tiburon as "a bundle of tracks and a clump of smoky buildings and 42 acres of land . . . a workshop of noise, oil, welding, and hammering."

During these years residents of Tiburon — whether they worked for the railroad or not — felt the sure conviction that they lived in a real railroad town. For them, the sound of a train, especially in the middle of the night, was the most familiar and dependable sound of all. Four freight trains a day rumbled in, with twenty-five or more cars on each, pulled first by woodburners, then by oilburning engines, and finally by diesels. The Tiburon shops could build or repair just about anything, from the magnificent ferryboats to handcars.

Gradually trains disappeared from the Tiburon scene. The turntable for locomotives was dismantled in 1958, and the shops were phased out over the next years as repair work was shifted to the parent (since 1929) Southern Pacific. The last shops in the Tiburon yards were closed September 30, 1963. A single operation was left at Tiburon: handling freight cars barged by Santa Fe across the bay to and from Richmond and San Francisco.

This lasted until 1967, when on September 25 at 10:15 a.m. the last barge tied up and discharged eight freight cars loaded with building materials, furniture, and beer. The cars were attached to a diesel locomotive and departed — the last train out of Tiburon. It had been 83 years, four months, and 24 days since Peter Donahue's May Day excursion.

Frank Smith, who delivered packages for Railway Express, seemed pleased with his job and proud of his Model-T truck when his picture was taken sometime in the 1920's. (Courtesy of Mrs. Mary Emma Kay)

Top: Riveting steel sills for new flat cars at the Tiburon shops, April, 1924. (Preston H. Kane Collection)

Opposite: Preston H. Kane, extreme left, helps demonstrate a new fire car built to his design at the Tiburon shops. The danger of a fire was always present in a railroad yard, and sparks from the wood-burning engines would sometimes set the timbers on the inside of the tunnels on fire.

Eleven locomotives at once could be hoisted overhead on huge racks for inspection and servicing in the Tiburon roundhouse. (Courtesy of the Bancroft Library)

The trestle, which crossed Tiburon Blvd. and eased up to the first tunnel, was a landmark for 84 years, until it was torn down in 1968, a year after the last train rumbled over its sturdy wooden framework. The pictures opposite are from the 1930's. By the 1950's (right), the scene had changed.

The diesel-electric locomotive in this 1958 photo weighed 325,000 pounds and was lifted by a Whiting hoist in the Tiburon shop. (Courtesy of Fred J. Buscher)

The Tiburon depot, where home-bound Marin commuters rattled their newspapers and listened for the "All Aboard!" from the train conductor.

Santa Fe barges were a familiar sight on the Tiburon waterfront for decades. The vertical assembly for hoisting the apron is called the gallows frame. This slip, the last on the waterfront, was dismantled in 1974. (Photo by Anna-Jean Cole, 1961)

The crew of the Motive Power and Car Department at the Tiburon yards in 1958. The Tiburon men are identified as (bottom row) third from left, Ernest Locati; fourth, Charles Pastori, Jr.; (second row standing) second from left, Waldo Ericson, visiting from the mechanical department; fifth from left, Raymond Albertini; extreme right, Fred J. Buscher, general foreman; (top row), third from left, Hugo Cattani; fifth, Matt Grbac. (Courtesy of Fred. J. Buscher)

(Photo: Anna Jean Cole)

In August, 1965, only rubble remained of the huge roundhouse with its eleven locomotive racks.

(Photo: Anna Jean Cole)

The Last Day

The Last Day
On September 25, 1967, the last freight train left Tiburon, almost 84 years after the first train, full of merry passengers, had made the trip to San Rafael. Apparently only Dorothy Carter happened to be there with a camera to record the historic event.

A few months later, the iron gallows frame, used to raise and lower the apron, and the huge ferry slip originally built for the Ukiah were demolished and carted away. (Philip Molten, Photographer)

In 1968, workmen began taking up the last railroad track in Tiburon. Again, only chance brought an observer by with a camera.
(Courtesy Louise Teather)

In March, 1984, just six weeks short of the hundredth anniversary of Donahue's opening day, one could hear again the roar of machines and the hubbub of construction in the railroad yards. Some 20,000 cubic yards of soil, containing layers of oil and deposits of lead from the days of the railroad, were removed and replaced by clean fill. Developers leveled a 38-acre site for a luxurious condominium complex, to be called Point Tiburon. Only the old depot remains as a substantial reminder of the railroad in Tiburon's past.
(Philip Molten, Photographer)

Northwestern Pacific train No. 3, coming in from Eureka, steams toward the Tiburon yards. The engineer pulls the cord of his steam whistle. A little girl waves back. This picture represents a memory many people in Tiburon hold dear. (Courtesy Louise Teather)

The NWP lantern was found in a ditch
by Dave Teather; the glass chimney
was recovered undamaged from the bottom
of the cove by diver Dave Benoit.
(Philip Molten, photographer)

Here is what a Main Street is for: a place for the whole community to meet on special occasions. This one is Flag Day, June 12, 1976. (Photo: Louise Teather)

Main Street

Tiburon surely has one of the shortest Main Streets in America: one block of straight thoroughfare, just 475 feet long, which bangs into Corinthian Island, makes a sharp right to skirt the island, then turns right again for a short run to Beach Road.

There is good reason for its brevity and apparent illogic. Main Street was built on a narrow gravelly spit connecting Point Tiburon and the island now called Corinthian. Until fairly recently, there was water on both sides. The straight section running from the island to Beach Road was a drawbridge through which boats and arks could enter and leave the old lagoon.

The first buildings along the little spit faced the bay, with their backs resting on pilings in the lagoon. The south side of the street remained an empty beach for forty years, except for a few small shacks and one large two-story building with five oddly spaced windows on each floor, which appears in the earliest photograph, taken about 1883. Judging from its size, it was probably a hotel.

Another hotel and some rooming houses sprang up across the street to house the four hundred Irish railroad workers who poured into Point Tiburon in about 1883 to build the railroad and ferry slips. The *Sausalito News* in the mid-1880's reports:

> Point Tiburon rose to the dignity of its first trial by jury on last Monday. It seems that on Saturday night the captain of the schooner Sycamore was shaking the dice with some of his friends at the new hotel when one Mr. Martin made some remarks about the game which irritated the captain and he told Martin to shut up, whereupon the latter used some very insulting language. The captain immediately knocked him down, and Martin subsequently got out a warrant for his arrest from Justice McLaughlin. The case was tried on Monday before a jury who found the captain guilty but recommended him to the mercy of the court. A fine of $20 and costs of court was imposed but it is stated that the case will be taken to the Superior Court on appeal.

By 1884, the year when the first train steamed down the new track, Tiburon had become a real town with a post office established May 28, and a polling place at Savage's Hotel where 44 residents voted in November, with 33 votes cast for a new president, Grover Cleveland.

Grocery stores, boarding houses, stables, dry-goods stores, and of course saloons appeared along Main Street in the next few years. In 1889, when Marin County began issuing licenses to saloons, four were granted to Tiburon, to Michael O'Brien, Paul Sire, William O'Connor, and S.W. Ohm. (In Sausalito, twenty licenses were issued).

The rowdy railroad builders who patronized the saloons were followed in the 1890's by more staid middle-class employees with families. St. Hilary's church, built in 1888, was a white mark of respectability on the hill above town. Portuguese and Italian dairy workers came to town to buy shirts and dresses for their families, and to sample the sweets and ice cream in the confectionary. Yachtsmen from the new Corinthian Yacht Club shopped for groceries and supplies for their boats. Tourists came to rent boats, arks, and cottages from C.A. McNeil's Pioneer Boat House. Islanders from Belvedere crossed the drawbridge on their way from the ferry to their elegant new houses, sometimes stopping for a little refreshment along the way.

Main Street was lined with wagons and carts drawn by draft horses from the dairy farms, with here and there a smart Victoria or a Petaluma buggy with a team of sleek matched bays or blacks. The grocer, who was obliged to deliver his goods, kept his own cart and horse in a stable next to the store.

The street took on an almost international flavor: a person could patronize not only McNeil's boathouse, but Max Bernstein's shaving parlor, Polichek's restaurant, Tsukimoto's laundry, Sullivan's saloon, and Hansen's liquor store.

The *Sausalito News*, on January 16, 1897, had some carefully qualified praise for the little village:

TIBURON
Not Beautiful to Look Upon but Full of Energy

Belvedereites when going from their homes to the ferry have to pass through Tiburon, their shopping place. Tiburon is not what might be called a pretty place, but there are few of its size in California which can compare with it in enterprise, and the efforts of

A very early picture of Main Street, about 1884, shows the Tiburon Hotel and Saloon and a large building on the south side which wins the prize for survival: it's still there. (Courtesy Joseph A. Baird, Jr.) A view from the Corinthian Yacht Club shows a brand new church on the hill (1888) and the hotel floated down from Sonoma County (far right).

the citizens to advance the interests of the town are worthy of emulation by larger and more settled communities. The citizens are as one large harmonious family. The welfare of one is the welfare of all. Several times during the past summer they have combined and extended free-handed hospitality to all who might come and eat of the justly celebrated Tiburon clams. The town is distinctly a commercial one, and the shops of the Donahue railroad being situated there give an air of bustle to the place which is not assumed but real. The growth of Belvedere will materially help to advance the interests of Tiburon, and the energetic merchants of the place will not be slow to take advantage of it. Some of the most prominent are Jerry O'Connell, a school trustee, Sam McDonough, Judge Hayden, Fugit & Russell, C.J. Madison, W.C. Lewis, H. Fisher, C. McNeil, W.H. Fishbourne, Victor Beyries and Captain Brown.

The history of Main Street is difficult to trace because buildings were erected, enlarged, dismantled, moved, or disguised with bewildering rapidity. The whole town of Donahue on the Petaluma Creek — shops, boarding houses, and all — was dismantled and floated to Tiburon on barges. The Sonoma House, a two-story hotel with veranda that occupies a prominent place in early pictures of Donahue, arrived and took its place at the east end of Main Street with even its sign intact. Patrons who had made reservations for a room overlooking the Petaluma slough found themselves with a glorious view of Angel Island instead.

Fires, too, changed the face of Main Street. The small wooden buildings would go up in a flash, sometimes taking a neighbor or two along with them. On November 21, 1890, the *Sausalito News* reported:

On Thursday last one of the most serious conflagrations known for some time devastated the entire business portion of Tiburon. The fire seemed to have originated through a defective flue in the Tiburon Hotel kept by Wm. O'Connor. The stores in this quarter are all constructed of a matchwood material and very soon the fire gained such headway that all the heroic efforts of the inhabitants to stay its galloping progress proved futile. The entire loss is estimated at $25,000.

A large portion of the population were left houseless and had it not been for the kindly intervention of Superintendent Whiting who supplied blankets in the railroad cars, much suffering would have been caused, especially to the women and children. The Steamer J.M. Donahue, in endeavoring to approach near enough to throw a stream on the flames, owing to low tide got aground and was useless. The principal sufferers are H. Cookson, C. Ozan, Capt. Brown, T. Enright, S.W. Ohm, and the railroad company. The defunct stores were all built on leased land and erected in the cheapest and flimsiest manner possible.

Mr. O'Connor of the late Tiburon Hotel has already put in foundations and floor on which he has a large canvas square house where he received his patrons who were numbered by the thousands on Sunday last who went to Tiburon to see the effects of the great fire.

James Collins, Mike Morris, Joe Dutra and Peter Owler done commendable work at the late fire.

The respectable inhabitants of Tiburon complain much of the rowdy element existing here since the fire. There is a floating palace on which is held an all night carnival. We wish a limit as to hours could be enforced.

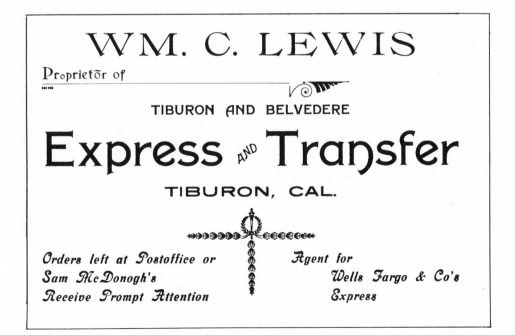

The Great Fire of Tiburon occurred on April 4, 1921, making page one news in the San Francisco papers. Nine-year-old Marjorie McNeil sounded the alert when she spotted the flames in Sullivan's, variously called a soft-drink parlor, pool hall, and saloon. Local firefighters had the help of the railroad fire crew and finally of a San Francisco engine company, eight men and a pump, who rushed across the bay on the ferryboat *Tamalpais*. But they were too late. The Tiburon Hotel, two grocery stores (the post office was in one of them), the butcher shop, garage, haberdashery, two confectionaries, and a barbershop-poolroom all burnt to the ground.

When Main Street was rebuilt after the fire, some old arks took their place in the row. Buildings rose on the south side as well as the north, and the street began to close itself off from the Bay. An imposing brick and stone bank appeared at the end of the street.

Part of the lore of Main Street has to do with the saloons and those who visited them: railroad "gandy-dancers," sailors from the coaling station, soldiers from Angel Island, and seamen from the codfishery on the west side of the Belvedere Island who sang sea chanties as they walked back over the hill.

As a seafaring and railroading town located at the end of a long peninsula with one road in, and a lookout point from which unwanted callers coming by sea could be spotted a long way off, Main Street didn't have to be any better than it wanted to be. During Prohibition, liquor from Canada and Europe was unloaded into small boats from ships anchored outside the three-mile limit, then brought into coastal towns under cover of darkness or fog. Some say that Tiburon was a center for bootlegging, with secret concrete storage rooms under the buildings on the Bay side of Main Street. One story says that whiskey was even stored in the bank's vault.

From 1909 onward, when all passenger traffic was diverted to Sausalito and the great ferries stopped pouring out passengers into town, Main Street began to settle into a comfortable middle age. In the 1920's the street was paved, and some years later sidewalks replaced the wooden planks and gravel paths. The grocer scrapped his buggy and bought a Model T.

Slowly the lagoon filled in with silt and mud dredged from the bottom of the coves by the railroad and the yacht clubs. The drawbridge was replaced with a solid concrete span; then even that was filled in, and salt water no longer flowed into the lagoon to cleanse it. Open water became marsh, and marsh became mudflat under the summer sun.

Like many small towns, Tiburon simply dug in and held its own during the 30's and 40's. The peninsula was still a cow pasture with a Main Street and a train yard. Buildings were allowed to run down. The original railroad crewmen were grandfathers now, and a new generation of men, much sobered by the Great Depression, tended the locomotives and freightcars.

One of the few evidences of progress was that the Tiburon road was paved and made a direct route to the east end of Main Street. (Before that, travellers turned right at San Rafael Avenue, drove along the east shore of Belvedere, turned onto Beach Road and crossed the drawbridge in order to reach Main Street.)

After World War II, new people moved to Tiburon, and the town began its evolution into a bedroom suburb of San Francisco, thanks partly to the Golden Gate Bridge. But this evolution was relatively slow, because of the town's location at the tip of a peninsula; even today, there is an inherent illogic in *driving* to San Francisco.

As the cow pastures shrank and housing developments boomed in the 1950's, little Main Street seemed outmoded and forlorn. Businesses moved to the new Boardwalk shopping center, which had a huge parking lot. Main Street's last grocery (Beyries') closed in September, 1955.

Even the post office moved to a new building to be combined with the Belvedere post office. Souvenir shops and cafes remained to serve tourists, many of whom arrived by boat. But the street looked hopelessly old-fashioned, and the bent of the fifties was to expand, modernize, and streamline. People looked to the future; they wanted to forget the war and the depression years.

Community leaders began to worry about the future of Main Street. Then in September, 1955, one resident, Constance Field, suggested that the whole town join together to paint the weathered storefronts. In a single festive weekend, dozens of volunteers put on their old clothes and painted the fronts of fifteen buildings. When they were finished, the street had a new, spruced-up look; people could see that there was a kind of homey, familiar charm here that no shopping center could duplicate.

Years later, people realized that the "Paint-Up" marked the turning point in Tiburon's change from a railroad town to the commuter-tourist community of today.

In 1956 Fred G. Zelinsky, a weekend resident and prominent San Francisco painting contractor (he donated the scaffolding and the services of two trim painters to the Paint-Up), became the major property owner on Main Street. He restored or rebuilt the buildings along the street's second block, calling it Ark Row because several old arks set up on pilings were interspersed with old summer cottages along the curve of Corinthian Island.

A resident of fifty years ago would know just where he was today: on a street that is like a long, expansive, comfortable room with one end open and corridors leading out to magnificent views of the bay and the city.

By 1890, cottages lined the back of Corinthian; the rooming houses brought down from Donahue Landing are perfectly aligned at left, and the old lagoon, now a parking lot, is smooth as glass. The shingle cottage with odd windows is still there in 1984 (right and below.)

(Philip Molten, Photographer)

This splendid picture, from about 1895, has much to tell about early Tiburon. The parade is on its way to the drawbridge to see the yachts and arks come out of the lagoon for the summer. The occasion is a formal one: note the plug hats, with here and there a straw sailor. Some of the celebrants ride in horse-drawn omnibuses. The street is unpaved but smooth; it seems to have been cleaned for the parade. Plank sidewalks and a row of wooden awnings line the north side. On the south the two-story building has a new wide awning of its own, the first of many disguises. At the far end of the street two very small buildings, distinctly non-conformist, sport false fronts with cornices. The photographer is perched on the balcony of the Sonoma House Hotel, brought down from Donahue Landing in 1887.

(Courtesy Herbert Stone)

Two pictures present a puzzle in history: how would you date them? The cars and a truck unloading Mother's Bread are clues; yet a pony cart is loaded with parcels, and buggies abound. Two small shops shown in the upper picture have been replaced by a large, hip-roofed building. There is a new restaurant in town. To the right of the hotel a little false-front building has been widened, presumably by someone named Burke.

The Hansen Saloon is ready for business in 1900. No one was drinking at ten minutes to two in the afternoon. Note five spigots on the right, Hansen's name in gilt over the bar, a nickelodeon at left. (Courtesy Bancroft Library.)

(Roy Graves Collection)

N. R. HANSEN

Private Rooms for Ladies and Families

Hot Tamales and all kinds of Cold Lunches

 Family Liquor Store

Sandwiches Served

Ice Cold Steam and Lager

Full Line in Cigars, Wines and Liquors

Furnished Rooms

TIBURON, MARIN CO., CAL.

Top: Main Street looks crowded in this panorama, circa 1901. The Sonoma House hotel is visible at the far right. The Pioneer Boat House had plenty of business in this most peaceful of modern eras.

Advertisements are from 1899.

The huge steamer Ukiah is docked at the long wharf in this view, also taken about 1901. The square white house above it is still there, although much altered. At far left is the Tiburon school (1901).

(Courtesy Dick Williamson)

Two views of Main Street taken sometime after the Great Fire of 1921; most of the buildings along the street survive today. The cars and clothes suggest that the top picture was taken in the middle 1920's, the other about five years later, after the street was paved. As these pictures show, cars were beginning to take over the street.

(Courtesy California Historical Society)

In this view, taken in the late 1940's (note the 1947
Chevy and Plymouth), we see the same building we saw
in the 1884 picture on p. 78. It has a new roof, cornice,
and stepped facade, perhaps because of damage suffered
in the 1921 fire.

Main Street today has kept many of the same facades
on the north side. The power lines have been put
underground.

(Philip Molten, Photographer)

This panorama was taken in 1955, just two months before the Paint-Up that transformed Main Street, which was looking very weary. Two of the buildings on the south side of the street are old arks on pilings. Musso's Bakery is on the corner.

91

Lots of children and dogs and sunshine appeared for the great Paint-Up of Tiburon's Main Street in September, 1955. Volunteers put on old clothes and caps, and happily splashed paint on the weatherbeaten buildings. At the end of two days many people in town had come to realize how much Main Street meant to them.

Main Street in 1977. The facades are familiar,
except for two new buildings built in the old style,
on the far left. The street has been furnished with
handsome (and expensive) gas lights, probably
much more elegant than anything used here in
the old days.

(Philip Molten, Photographer)

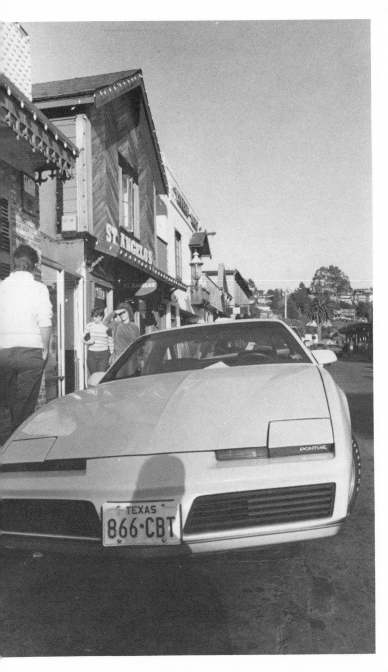

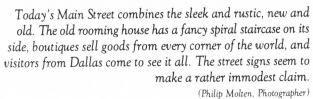

Today's Main Street combines the sleek and rustic, new and old. The old rooming house has a fancy spiral staircase on its side, boutiques sell goods from every corner of the world, and visitors from Dallas come to see it all. The street signs seem to make a rather immodest claim.

(Philip Molten, Photographer)

On Sept. 9, 1864, the brigantine Timandra anchored in the middle of Belvedere Cove and the schooner Alert put down her anchor in the old lagoon, about where Bon Appetit is today. The Timandra had brought codfish from the Okhotsk Sea and the Alert's smaller cargo was from the Bering Sea. In the lithograph above, sailors are seen taking fish ashore for curing and packing on the site now occupied by the San Francisco Yacht Club. By coincidence, five years later the artist, Captain Edwin Moody, was one of the founders of the club. (Courtesy Bancroft Library)

Beach Road

Beach Road in Belvedere and Main Street in Tiburon are like fraternal twins. Far from identical, they still share a common history, having grown up side by side; their coloring is different, but they are inseparably bound together for life.

Like Main Street, Beach Road was originally a gravel spit reaching out from Belvedere (then called Still Island) toward Corinthian (which had no name at all). A tidal channel at the east end, deep enough to allow passage of fairly sizable sailing vessels, led into the old lagoon.

The first real settler, a forty-niner from Ohio, arrived in 1855. Israel Kashow, six foot three and 250 pounds, was tough, quick-tempered, independent. He liked "Kashow's Island," as he called it, and stubbornly stuck to it for thirty years, despite being repeatedly advised that it was actually a peninsula belonging to the Reed grant. One story tells that Kashow was accused of digging a wide trench across the natural causeway (San Rafael Avenue), to make Belvedere into an island and thus detach it from the grant.

Israel and his wife Elizabeth built a house where the San Francisco Yacht Club is today, planted a garden and orchard, and raised a large family, resisting all efforts to dislodge them, despite a "complaint of ejectment" filed in 1868 by the Reed heirs. In 1868, the U.S. Army declared the island a military reservation, remaining discreetly neutral in the Kashow-Reed battle by calling the site "Peninsula Island."

After a decade of privacy on the island, the Kashows acquired a neighbor. Nicholas Bichard, a pioneer San Francisco ship owner and merchant in coal, lumber, codfish and junk, had come to California in 1850, when he was twenty years old. After the Civil War Bichard and Kashow became partners in a fishyard. For years Bichard's ships sailed north every spring and brought back codfish to be cured and packed at Kashow's plant, at about No. 36 Beach Road.

Bichard, who was "passionately fond of the sea," preferred to live on board ship even when on dry land. He lived for several years in the cabin removed from the old Pacific Mail sidewheeler China in 1886 when the fine old steamer went to her fate at the hands of wreckers. The San Francisco Examiner in 1893 described Bichard as "a short, stout, jovial old fellow," living in his elegant cabin with its spotless white paint, gilded trim, and bearskin rugs.

Convinced that others would share his passion for shipboard living, Bichard created an "entire collection of queer dwellings" from the hulks of old vessels placed along the beach and on the lagoon side, too. Shacks were made of timbers and doors from old ships. Cottages were built on top of boat hulls either floating or set up on pilings. Bichard became the first architect of Beach Road as a community, for his cottages attracted a colorful, rather Bohemian populace.

When the island was declared indisputably part of the Rancho Corte Madera in 1885, Kashow was forced to leave. But he had in his pocket the deeds to 139 acres of tidelands, bought in the 1871 tidelands auctions, 89 of them surrounding Beach Road, Main Street, and most of Corinthian Island.

Kashow is credited with building the first drawbridge, in 1888, across the channel between Beach Road and Corinthian; until then people had to row or swim across.

For many years the raising of the bridge in the fall for arks and sailboats to pass into the old lagoon for winter anchoring, and again in the spring for them to come out, were festive affairs, viewed by hordes of spectators. The spring event marked the start of the yachting season, and was the forerunner of the modern Opening Day on the Bay.

But for festivity the annual Night in Venice couldn't be surpassed. This was a water festival modeled on an ancient Venetian tradition, with the whole community, small as it was then, joining in. Residents decorated their houses, sailboats, and arks with strings of lanterns.

The newspapers exhausted their supplies of superlatives to describe the fireworks, water sprayed from fireboats, and the grand parade of lighted boats. In 1895 the Chronicle reported that the entertainment was to be an "exclusive" affair, with the invitations "limited to 5,000."

While Beach Road was never a truly commercial street, some businesses have made it their home. In the early 1890's the first Belvedere Hotel, consisting of just two cottages (one possibly Kashow's old house), opened on the cove. It was the peninsula's first tourist attraction. This modest inn was succeeded in 1898 by a rustic four-story building also called the Belvedere Hotel, which cost $10,000 and had fifty rooms. The hotel flourished over the turn of the century and then languished, to be replaced in 1934 by the San Francisco Yacht Club.

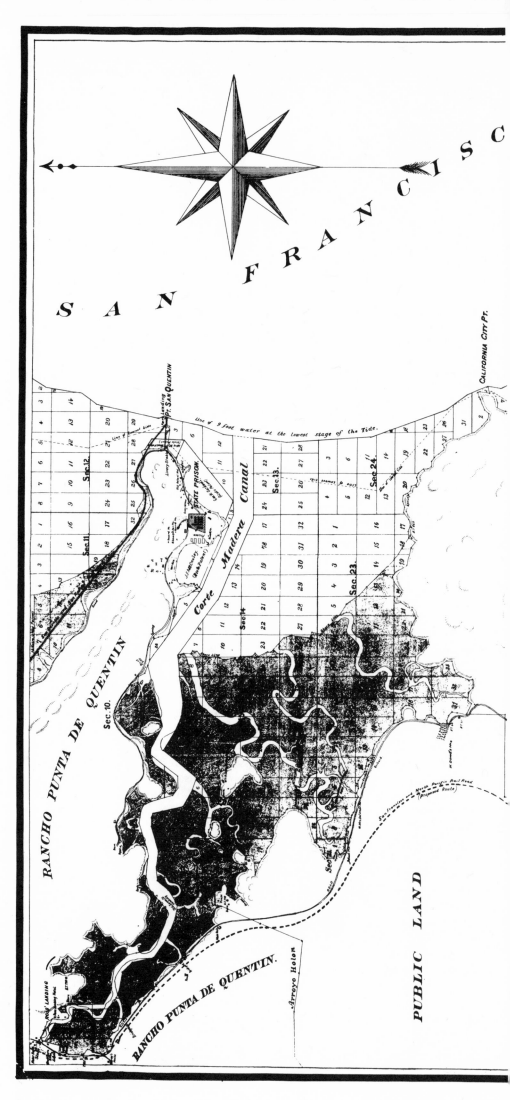

The Tidelands Map, published just before the auction in 1871. The tidelands were deemed outside the boundaries of the Rancho Corte madera, and were available to the highest bidder. Israel Kashow, who had lived on "Kashow's Island" (here called "Peninsula Island" with a fine disregard for logic) for sixteen years, was a prominent bidder at the auction. He secured title to 139 acres of tidelands, 89 of them adjacent to Beach Road, Corinthian Island, and the future Main Street of Tiburon. Although he was eventually driven off the island itself by the heirs of John Reed, Kashow kept his watery property; during eighty years of leases many of the lots changed from water to land. Kashow's heirs sold the property in the 1950's. (Courtesy Bancroft Library)

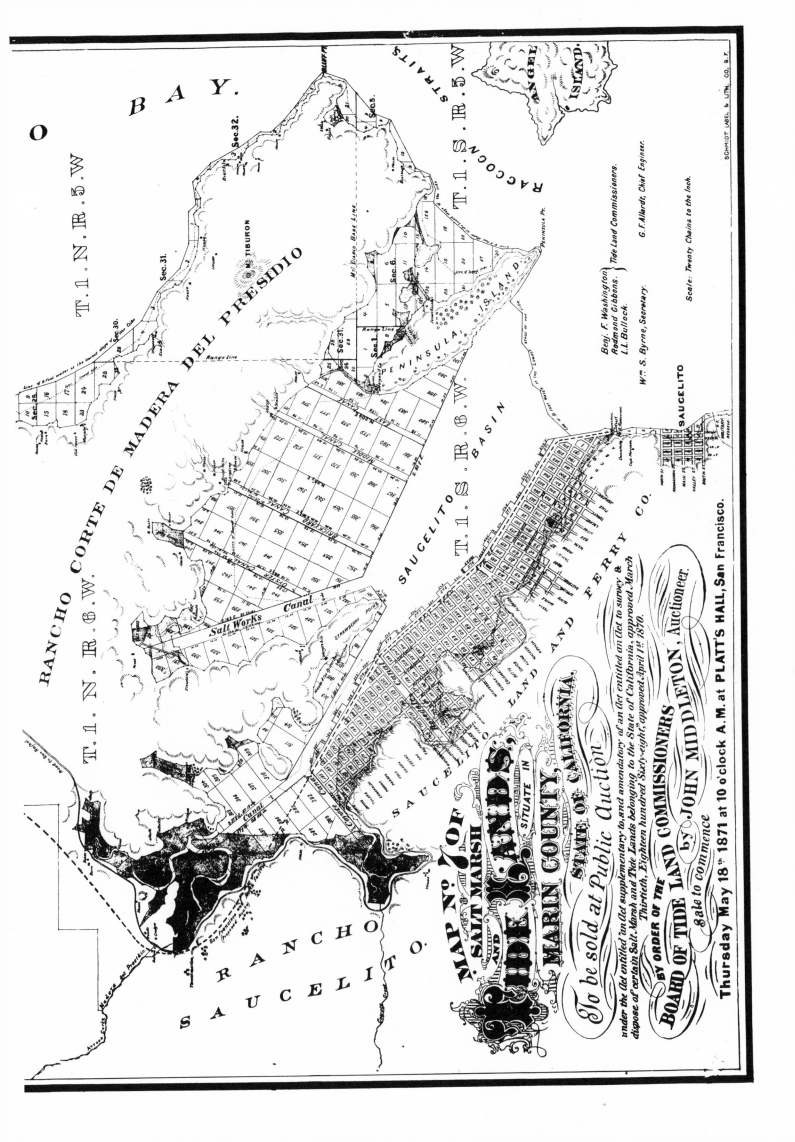

O BAY.

O

T.1.N. R.5.W.

Sec.32.

Sec.31.

TIBURON

Sec.30.

Sec.31.

Sec.25.

RANCHO CORTE DE MADERA DEL PRESIDIO

T.1.N. R.6.W.

T.1.N. R.6.W.

Mt. Diablo Base Line

Sec.31.

Sec.6

Range Line

Sec.1

Range Line

RACCOON STRAITS

T.1.S. R.5.W.

ANGEL ISLAND.

PENINSULA ISLAND.

Peninsula Pt.

SAUCELITO BASIN

T.1.S. R.6.W.

SAUCELITO

EAST CANAL

MIDDLE CANAL

BRICKYARD CANAL

Salt Works Canal

Strawberry Point

SAUCELITO LAND AND FERRY CO.

RANCHO SAUCELITO.

RANCHO SAUCELITO.

SCHMIDT LABEL & LITH. CO. S.F.

Benj. F. Washington Tide Land Commissioners.
Rodmond Gibbons.
L.L. Bullock.

Wm. S. Byrne, Secretary.

G.F.Allardt, Chief Engineer.

Scale: Twenty Chains to the Inch.

MAP No. 2 OF
SALT MARSH
AND
TIDE LANDS,
SITUATE IN
MARIN COUNTY,
STATE OF CALIFORNIA,

under the Act entitled "an Act supplementary to, and amendatory of an Act entitled an Act to survey &
dispose of certain Salt-Marsh and Tide Lands belonging to the State of California, approved March
Thirtieth, Eighteen hundred Sixty-eight", approved April 1st 1870.

BY ORDER OF THE
BOARD OF TIDE LAND COMMISSIONERS
by JOHN MIDDLETON, Auctioneer.
To be sold at Public Auction
Sale to commence

Thursday May 18th 1871 at 10 o'clock A.M. at PLATT'S HALL, San Francisco.

The bearded Patriarch: Israel Kashow, resident of Kashow's Island (Belvedere) 1855-1885. (Courtesy of the Kashow family)

The prow of the old ship Tropic Bird with a two-story addition was a duplex on Beach Road for many years. The China Cabin is just behind it. Farther along the beach in this 1890's picture are two cottages which comprised the first Belvedere Hotel, left of center. On the hill above are some early Belvedere houses, including the Pagoda House.

Opposite, below: Lester Stone, 4 years old, with a friend in 1896 at the boat yard on Beach Road operated by his father, W.F. Stone. The yacht Nixie is on the ways. Lester Stone grew up to be a noted yachtsman as well as boatbuilder. (Photo courtesy of his sister, Ethel Stone O'Grady)

The tranquil surface of Belvedere Cove in 1895, where thirteen grown-ups, all sporting hats, have crowded into one rowboat; six men perch precariously on the gunwales, to wait for the opening of the bridge to the lagoon. On the beach in the center background are the two cottages comprising the Belvedere Hotel.

OLD NICK IS NO MORE.

Sudden Death of Captain Bichard.

He Was a Character of the Coast.

Story of His Mania for Old Ships, Marine Junk and Such Things.

Big, bluff old Captain "Nick" Bichard, whose arks fringe the Tiburon spit, is no more. He had been ailing for some time, but nobody believed him to be dangerously ill. He came to San Francisco on Thursday, transacted some business and then returned to his queer little home on the bay. Before he retired for the night he complained of feeling ill, but as he had not been in the best of health of late little more than passing solicitude was expressed for the old seafaring man. When morning broke "Old Nick," as he was familiarly known by his chums about the spit and in town, did not respond to his daughter's call to breakfast. His door was opened and he was found apparently asleep with one arm outstretched and the other resting beneath his head. A vigorous shaking did not arouse "Old Nick," and then it was discovered that his slumber was past awakening. He had died some time during the night, with his favorite sea beating a monotone in his ears. The distracted daughter aroused the neighborhood, and in a few moments the chamber, which is just above the water, was filled with mourners.

"Nick" Bichard was a good deal of a man in his day. Born in the Isle of Guernsey in November, 1830, he early became passionately fond of the sea. He came to California in 1850 and engaged in the lumber business, in which he was immensely successful. During the Civil War he was a heavy Government contractor and built the barracks at the Presidio. Then his old love for the sea becoming irresistible he bought and equipped eight vessels and sent them to the northern waters for fish, coal and lumber. It was about twenty years ago that he established a fish yard at Tiburon and thither his vessels came after their catches. For a time Bichard continued to add to the savings he had made in the lumber business and from his contracts with the Government. Then like the storms that swept over his beloved sea reverses came thick and fast. His vessels went down one after the other until but two were left—the schooners Don Carlos and Don Adolphus, which are now flying the Chilean flag. While at the zenith of his prosperity "Nick" Bichard's

wealth was reckoned at $500,000, and there is now many a gray beard in Tiburon who used to smoke his short pipe along the shore and discuss the daring and success of the mariner.

Misfortune, however, did not crush the spirit of the energetic man. When his splendid fortune had been all but swept away he adopted new business tactics. Securing the Tiburon spit on a series of long leases he began to colonize it with all the old hulks he could find in the graveyards of the bay. These he moored to the shore, jacked them up on piles and afterward converted them into houses and

the deep, and yesterday children clamored in and out of the oddly constructed houses and stared at the black wagon of the undertaker as it stood before the cottage of the old captain. All about the spit lay the strange purchases of the man who found something of worth in every fixture of an abandoned ship. There were capstans and spars and wheels, and chains and ropes enough to fill a chandler's loft. Sometimes "Old Nick" would sell these scraps at a profit, and with this revenue and that which he derived from his two ships and the rentals of his colony of cottages,

"OLD NICK" BICHARD, THE FAMOUS CHARACTER OF TIBURON, WHO WAS FOUND DEAD IN HIS BED.

arks. If tenants wanted them furnished "Old Nick" would get the carpets, chairs and things and then come around in the evening and tell the children of the householders stories of his life as a sea captain along the South American coast. The man's mania for buying dismantled ships and the junk they contained was something extraordinary. He made a lodging-house out of the old Sacramento-river steamer Flora Temple and converted the hull of the ever-famous Tropic Bird into a cottage whose seaward porch still holds the bowsprit and chains of the pride and the hope of the Argonauts. Within a few years "Old Nick" had the spit lined with these veterans of

he managed to live in apparent comfort. He was no longer rich, but his lot was far better than that of many of the rugged fellows who used to sit around him and spin yarns about the good old codfish days and the time when he lugged coal and lumber on his fleet from the north and along the South American coast.

The autopsy held yesterday revealed the fact that "Old Nick" had died of fatty degeneration of the heart. He was also possessed of an abnormal liver. The body was brought to San Francisco last night and early to-morrow morning it will be taken to the cemetery. Mr. Bichard's wife died about twelve years ago. He leaves a daughter and one son.

The interior of the China Cabin when Nicholas Bichard lived there boasted "unspotted white paint and gilding," and the floors were covered with "costly carpets and bearskins", the Examiner reported in 1893. Bichard evidently collected Indian baskets.

This very rare picture shows a "Night in Venice" festival in the 1890's. (Courtesy Phil Franks)

A peaceful turn-of-the-century scene: arks and sailboats in Belvedere Cove; the big, rustic Belvedere Hotel (extreme left) and a variety of other buildings along Beach Road. On the opposite shore, a dairy barn is the only sign of habitation on the empty Tiburon hills, and a few more arks are tied up below Red Hill. (Courtesy of the Society of California Pioneers)

In the 1920's artists rented the Beach Road cove-side cottages. Gottardo Piazzoni, known as the dean of Bay Area artists and a noted teacher, moved with his family to a house next door to the China Cabin. The Piazzonis' friends and neighbors were the sculptor Ralph Stackpole and his family. The landscape painter Seldon Gile rented a cottage and studio on Beach Road in 1943. A cache of his paintings, which today are exceedingly valuable, was found there after his death in 1946.

After World War II Beach Road began to lose its haphazard look. The old lagoon, which had become a mosquito-infested mudflat closed off from the bay, was dredged by the Belvedere Land Company and the resultant silt was made into long fingers of land on which houses were built. Salt water entered the lagoon again, and the tides cleaned away scum and mosquito breeding grounds. Old cottages were moved from Beach Road to new locations behind the Boardwalk, and handsome apartment buildings rose to take in the incomparable view of San Francisco.

The jewel of Beach Road today, just as in the 1890's, is the China cabin, nearing the completion of a half-million-dollar restoration financed by the National Trust, various foundations, and private contributors. Large openings on the south side of the street allow the stroller to see the same beach where Israel Kashow and Nicholas Bichard dried codfish a hundred years ago.

(Courtesy Herbert Stone)

The east end of Beach Road sometime after the turn of the century. The bones of an old ship at right are those of the side-wheeler Flora Temple, which during the 1890's served as a social hall, church, and the area's first library.
The large square building facing the bridge was the home in 1943 of Seldon Gile, an important California artist. The building, much altered, remains in place in 1984 (right).

105

Waves pounded against the Belvedere Hotel
and cottages on Beach Road in the 1921 storm.

On Christmas Day 1921, a fierce storm struck the area. "We were
awakened by the sound of strong wind and rain whipping,
pounding, and whistling against our house", recalls a resident of the
cottage next door to the China Cabin. The Cabin was hit by boats
blown from their anchorage, and forced off its pilings; after the
storm it was placed on a new foundation closer to the road. (Photo
courtesy of the Belvedere Land Co.)

Watercolor by Robert Bastian of Corinthian Island and Red Hill, with Beach Road and Belvedere Cove in the foreground, about 1948. (Courtesy of Mrs. Harrison McClung)

For help with your car in the early 1920's you telephoned the Belvedere Garage on Beach Road, 37-J in the daytime and 37-W at night.

A man with a leg hooked over the railing of the ark Nautilus *awaits a caller approaching in a rowboat in Belvedere Cove in 1899. He is presumably James McNeil, who in 1894 paid $38 for four old Market Street horsecars, nailed them to a raft, and dubbed the result the* Nautilus. *The cozy interior (left) didn't lack for seating or windows.*

The Arks

In the early 1890's, a jaunty floating population appeared in Belvedere Cove: a flotilla of arks, or houseboats, which were moored in the cove from April until October, then towed into the shelter of the lagoon for the winter. In 1894, a reporter from the *Sausalito News* counted twelve of these unlikely vessels swaying from their anchors; by the turn of the century, the number had risen to thirty or forty.

They were of every conceivable description, from little more than Tom Sawyer rafts to elegant wood-panelled retreats, with elaborate upholstery. One, owned by a man named Wellington who had chosen this way of being prepared for the second flood, which he felt was imminent, was 62 feet long and had a glassed-in garden, presumably for raising food during those long forty days at sea.

More typically, an ark had four rooms and a kitchen, with hogsheads of water for drinking and washing. White railings circled the deck, and there were bunks everywhere for friends, who could be numerous, for many boats were owned jointly by several families.

One of the most original of these floating residences, the *Nautilus*, came into existence when James McNeil brought four abandoned horse-drawn San Francisco streetcars over on a barge towed by the ferry and nailed them to a raft. In 1895 the *Examiner* described McNeil's progress: "Down on the beach is a varied assortment of sash boards, doors, windows, some superfluous roofing and an assortment of wheels that were not found necessary for the comfort of ark life." One of the chief delights of the *Nautilus* must have been the number of windows.

An English newswoman, writing an account of Arktown for her magazine, *The Strand*, in 1899, could not refrain from remarking that the Belvedere boatowners neglected to line their deckhouses with potted flowers in the English manner, or lamenting that despite their awnings and chairs there was lacking "that cozy arrangement for afternoon tea which is such an important and pleasing feature of English boats." But she found much to admire:

> There is an indescribable charm about the life; one has the pleasures of boating combined with the comforts of home; sea baths are at one's very threshold; fish are caught and cooked while you wait. . . . The monotony of the scenery is varied by the swinging of the ark as it turns with the tide. There are neighbors, thirty or forty families of them, within easy reaching distance if one can pull a stroke, for there is always a following of rowboats lazily resting upon the water in the wake of each ark. The butcher, the baker, and others . . . who supply the needs of daily life each has his little boat which he sends around every morning for his customary order, and the joint for dinner and the ice cream for dessert are delivered as promptly to the ark-dwellers as they are to those who are still in the city.

The highlight of the summer season was the "Night in Venice," which featured concerts, fireworks, a torchlight procession of boats, open house on the arks, prizes for best decorations, and other festivities put on by the "Descendants of Noah," or "Venetians of the West," as the ark owners enjoyed calling themselves. One ark dweller, Lillian Saltonstall, recalled such a soiree in 1905:

> I remember particularly well one "Night in Venice." Belles and beaux were enjoying the scene and making love on the side. Finally, the moon began to wane, the music died away, and the lights went out. The "night" was over and the owners all went back to their own houseboats. We felt relaxed and happy. It had been an evening filled with gay social contacts, delicate dishes, and easy kisses.

When the drawbridge between the cove and the lagoon became a fixed span and the arks could no longer shelter in the lagoon during the winter, this era began to come to an end. Many of the remaining houseboats were put up on stilts and became cozy residences or rental cottages. Some were towed away to new locations in Sausalito or Larkspur; one very fine one, handsomely restored, is perched at the entrance to Bolinas Lagoon. Another has been restored for exhibition at the Hyde Street Pier in San Francisco.

Twelve members of an arkside swimming social in July, 1892, wear the fetching bathing costumes of the gay nineties.

June, 1892: the ark Mikado, owned by the George A. Crux family, carries a deckload of merry passengers, one of them toting a guitar.

The bedroom of the Crystal Palace, an elegant ark that James McNeil bought in 1895. Said the Sausalito News that year, "Mr. McNeil, through energy and hard work, has acquired quite a fortune. He can now boast of having the finest ark afloat. The furnishing and drapings of the interior are of the very best and the work of a first-class artist greets the visitor's eye upon the panels of the tasty natural wood finish." The dining room (below) displays more "tasty natural wood finish." The china cabinet testifies to McNeil's confidence in the placidity of the waters in Belvedere Cove, and the piano to his increasing wealth.

With mama at the tiller and papa on the oars, the Hugo Keil family is enroute to a houseboat outing, circa 1900. Far right is Tina, an orphan.

Goldberg Bowen delivered groceries to ark dwellers in 1899. Olive oil was apparently the only provision one needed for a picnic.

Seven old landlocked arks
living out their sunset years
at Beach and Cove Roads
were served eviction notices in
1968 to make room for the
Ark Apartments. The ark on
the left in the top picture was
donated to the Maritime
Museum by "ark angels"
Admiral and Mrs. Robert P.
Lewis. In April, 1969, the
Lewis ark was towed across
the bay to its new home on
The Hyde Street Pier. It is
now on exhibit there as an
example of the hundreds of
arks that once dotted the
sheltered coves of San
Francisco Bay. (Photos by
Anna-Jean Cole)

The other arks were relocated nearby, and are
now regarded as treasures by their lucky owners.

113

Since its first discovery by Spanish explorers in 1769, Angel Island has been everything from a refueling stop for whalers and otter-hunters, to a Mexican cattle ranch, American military base, prison camp for Arizona Indians, immigrant quarantine station, Nike missile base, and, by the time this photograph was taken in 1970, a California State Park.

To the left, on the east side of the island, we see East Garrison behind Point Simpton, Winslow Cove with a long dock extending into the water, Point Campbell, Ayala Cove, Point Ione, and, far right, Point Stuart. *(Courtesy Aero Photographers, Sausalito)*

Saving the Past for the Future

Imagine Tiburon as it might have looked today: with a roller coaster careening down the slopes of Angel Island, a housing development on filled-in Richardson Bay, apartment houses where Old St. Hilary's stands, a jutting fragment of rubble marking the site of Lyford's Stone Tower, and rows of houses where the bike path skirts the bay.

All of this could have happened. But it didn't, because thousands of people spent countless hours circulating petitions, attending meetings, collecting funds, and planning strategies in a thirty-year battle which is still being fought. The record of achievement is impressive; we can see the result every time we look out our windows.

Angel Island — since 1964 a part of incorporated Tiburon — was the object of much concern just after World War II, when the Federal Government was thinking of disposing of it and other fortified islands in the bay, perhaps to private developers.

Many people feared that the island might be turned into an amusement park, a sort of Disneyland North. A San Franciscan suggested that his city lease the island to a developer and share the profits, forgetting that Angel Island, except for Point Blunt, is in Marin County.

Other proposals were to use the island as a convention center, or as a tourist resort with casinos. The most ominous suggestion was to build a second bridge to Marin, leaping from the Embarcadero to Alcatraz to Angel Island to Tiburon, where a great new freeway would lead northward.

Alarmed residents of Marin, led by dedicated conservationist Caroline Livermore, organized in 1950 as the Angel Island Foundation, which persuaded the state to acquire the island from the Federal Government and preserve it.

The state obtained title to the site in stages, beginning with Ayala Cove in 1954; on September 26, 1970, Angel Island was dedicated as State Historical Landmark No. 529.

Old St. Hilary's Church, erected in 1888, was standing empty and forlorn on its grassy knoll in 1959, when its plight moved residents to found the Belvedere-Tiburon Landmarks Society, an organization dedicated to preserving the peninsula's historic heritage. St. Hilary's was purchased by the Landmarks Society that same year.

As it happened, the little white church also stood amidst what John Thomas Howell, botanist at the California Academy of Sciences, called "one of the most interesting and beautiful wildflower gardens in California, and thus in all the world." Private and public funds poured in, and today visitors not only can visit St. Hilary's, but can stroll among more than 200 plant species, many of them rare, in the John Thomas Howell Botanical Garden below the church.

On July 22, 1949, the *Independent-Journal* published a sketch showing a proposed real estate development at Richardson Bay. A corporation called Reedport Properties had bought up 879 acres of tidelands with the intention of filling in Richardson Bay to make 2,000 new homesites and a yacht harbor.

Six long years later, the Marin Conservation League and the Richardson Bay Foundation, led by Caroline S. Livermore, had raised more than $200,000 to buy the tidelands from the developers. When the dust settled, not only had the developers been stopped, but the Richardson Bay Wildlife Sanctuary had come into being to help protect the wildlife on land and water and to serve as an environmental education center.

Its headquarters, the Audubon Center of Northern California, was erected on land donated in 1957 by Rose Verrall, who gave the Audubon Society the nine-acre tract, her entire holdings, left to her in 1919 by a grandson of John Reed. That same year the Lyford house was barged across the cove, restored, and opened as a museum of the Victorian period. The house has become nationally famous.

In 1973, newspapers reported that developers were planning to plant 3,400 housing units on 770 acres of Ring Mountain on the north side of the Tiburon Peninsula. The alarm was sounded, and dozens of volunteers fought a long, ultimately successful campaign to save the mountain with its rare plants and intriguing geology as a nature preserve.

This effort was helped by the fortuitous sighting of the Tiburon Mariposa Lily, which grows only on Ring Mountain, and by the discovery there of Indian petroglyphs.

One of the most beloved landmarks of Tiburon's past stands beside Paradise Drive at the entrance to Lyford's Cove: a stone tower, built in 1889 by Benjamin Lyford as a gatehouse to his utopian development, Lyford's Hygeia.

A family picnic on the grass overlooking the officers' quarters at Camp Reynolds. Field cannon and piles of cannonballs line the parade ground in front of them. This fort was built on the west side of Angel Island in 1863 to prevent enemy ships — Confederate or otherwise — from slipping through Racoon Straits to attack the navy bases at Mare Island and Benicia. (Courtesy Bancroft Library)

Bottom: In this later picture, dated 1886, we see five cannon pointing at the strait from the beach at lower right. Below the chapel on the hill are officers' quarters; above is a fenced cemetery. A steamer is docked at the wharf. (Courtesy Presidio Army Museum)

Leaving their homes and villages,
they crossed the ocean
Only to endure confinement in
these barracks.
Conquering frontiers and barriers,
they pioneered
A new life by the Golden Gate
— Ngoot P. Chin

This is the English translation of the poem inscribed on a blue granite monument donated by Victor Bergeron in 1979. It was erected on the old Immigration Station on Angel Island as a tribute to the Chinese people.

(Philip Molten, Photographer)

Beginning around 1900, the East Garrison was an army training camp. At extreme left is the Paymaster's Office. Next was the Mess Hall, built in 1910, which could serve 1400 hungry soldiers at a time. At the end of the street, right of center, is the barracks, and the Post Exchange is at extreme right.

(Philip Molten, Photographer)

Built on Yerba Buena Island in 1860, "Quarters 11" was brought on a barge to Angel Island's West Garrison (Camp Reynolds), where it took its place as the eleventh house from the parade ground. Robert and Mary Noyes, with help from volunteers, finished restoring the building in 1983.

Now renovated, the 1863 bake house on the right is used by volunteers who bake bread there in the daytime and sleep there at night.

(Philip Molten, Photographer)

Lyford's Stone Tower was restored in 1980. Top: workmen install wire mesh on the inside of the tower before applying concrete. Bottom: reinforcing bars are bent to fit inside. This tower has stood on this rocky point for ninety years of sun, storm, fog, and occasional shaking of the earth. It was erected by Benjamin Lyford in 1889 as the southern gateway to one of California's first utopian communities. The tower is listed on the National Register.

The tower originally contained an office with fireplace. An archway and miniature tower were demolished when the road was widened in the 1920's, but the main tower remains, a fine example of Richardson Romanesque architecture and Victorian whimsy. The Tiburon Heritage Commission collected funds for its preservation. The tower was designated as a city landmark in 1974, and is listed on the National Register. Benjamin Lyford, who preserved things himself, would have approved.

The latest project of the Landmarks Society is the restoration of the China Cabin, a social saloon removed from the old Pacific Steamship Company sidewheeler *China* in 1886.

(Philip Molten, Photographer)

Old St. Hilary's was erected in 1888 to meet the
spiritual need of the railroad workers, who were
mostly Irish and Italian Catholics. Now owned
by the Landmarks Society, it shares its site with a
wildflower preserve.

(Photo: Anna Jean Cole)

Craftsmen meticulously restore the China Cabin,
the social salon that was removed from the sidewheeler China in 1886. Lower left: David
Brown. Right center: Louis de la Pena, Bruce
Allel, Al Giomi.

(Philip Molten, Photographer)

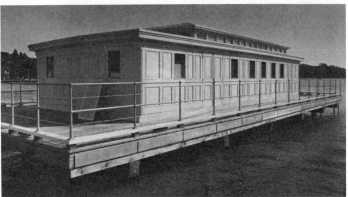

(Philip Molten, Photographer)

McKegney Green, dedicated in 1977, is used
principally for soccer, rugby, and picnicking.

Assemblyman Michael Wornum, Tiburon Councilman
Bruce Ross, and Mayor Donald Tayer, at the
dedication of McKegney Green.

Richardson Bay Path, which follows the old railroad right-of-
way along the shore, was dedicated on Oct. 9, 1971, by two
mayors on a tandem bike: Thomas Price of Belvedere, left,
and Denis Rice of Tiburon. At right are Bettye Allen and
Congressman William S. Mailliard. (Photo: Louise Teather)

122

A Handsome Bequest

In 1919 John Paul Reed, age 54, lived with his sister Clotilde at the Reed Ranch near Bel Aire. Rose Rodrigues (or Rogers) once Clotilde's servant, later John Paul's "dear friend," no longer visited the Reed Ranch; she lived alone on the north shore of Strawberry Point, spending her days baking bread, tending her garden, sawing wood, going to Mass, and caring for the goats and chickens that gave her her livelihood.

Rose kept a journal of her lonely life. A year had gone by "since I was insulted by my dear friend's sister," and Rose was heartsick at the rift this brought about between her and John Paul, who evidently took his sister's side in the quarrel. It had been a year since she last talked with him, although she often went by the ranch house hoping to get a glimpse of him on the porch. She prayed each day for a letter from him, but none ever came.

On Feb. 21, 1919, she writes in her diary, "In the afternoon I went to Mill Valley; just as I was leaving the place Mrs. Rita Borges and her sister were passing. Gave them a ride as far as the gate. My dear friend was on the porch. I suppose he thought I had men in the buggy with me but it was only women."

On May 4, 1918, John Paul had deeded Rose's ten-acre farm to her for $10. This may have provoked the quarrel with Clotilde, who would not even allow Rose in her house to receive a telephone call. On October 18, 1919, John Paul, who had long been ailing, had a gift deed delivered to Rose. He died the next month.

Rose never sold the ten-acre knoll that John Paul had given her. Before her death in 1964 she deeded the land as the site for the Audubon Center and the location for the Lyford house.

Rosie Verrall (1883-1964)

(Photo: Anna Jean Cole)

123

Benjamin and Hilarita Lyford lived in their two-story house from about 1876 to 1906. To the left of the house is the old ship's cabin which Dr. Lyford used as a laboratory for his embalming experiments.

After eight decades on Strawberry Point, the old Lyford House, threatened with demolition, was donated to the Marin Conservation League on condition that it be moved. The house was loaded on a barge and, on Dec. 4, 1957, towed free by Harbor Tugs a half mile across the bay to its new home at Rogers Beach, where it has been restored and opened as a Victorian museum.

Elegant and charming, the Lyford House is now a Victorian landmark at the Richardson Bay Audubon Center. The interior features a circular staircase with a banister of African mahogany, gold leaf trim, and etched glass skylights. (Photo: Philip Molten)

People, Places and Pastimes

The history of a town is more than the grand events — the coming of the Spanish ships, the sudden impact of a new mode of transportation, the utopian fantasy of the first man to lay out streets. These are important, but they are not the sum of our experience. The private lives, the names that no one can quite remember, the modest dwellings tucked away on the side of a hill — these too were once a part of the exuberant life of a place.

In this section, we see the faces of the people who have lived and worked in this place, strolled along the railroad tracks on the way to the ferry slip, squirmed before the camera of the school photographer, idled in a boat on the lagoon, felt in a green field the satisfying thunk of a baseball landing in a glove. The history of Tiburon is written in the faces of those who have kept its trains running, taught its children, put out its fires, healed its sick.

For people who live in a town that is "more water than land" the landscape too becomes a part of daily life and memory. In Tiburon people are always looking outward — at the bay, at islands, cities, bridges, boats, lowering clouds, fog. A glance out the window can make one forget what he was going to say, and that is often a blessing. The play of light on the beautiful mass of Mt. Tamalpais, a great flock of birds floating down on Richardson Bay — with such visions constantly before us we have some chance for perspective in a strident, confusing world.

Like Tiburon itself, this section is a mixture — an album of pictures chosen simply for the pleasure they give, and for what they show us about our own small occasions, which are very gradually becoming history.

John Bernard and Mary Borges were married at St. Hilary's Church in 1896 and lived on the Tiburon Peninsula most of their married lives. John, who had arrived from his native Azores as a teenager, worked at the Little Reed and Hilarita dairy ranches and then at Big Reed Ranch, where he was foreman. Their three children attended the first Reed School. (Courtesy of Mary Bernard Silva)

A class at the first Reed School in the 1890's. Is the little boy at the far left the same one we see to the far right in the picture below? If so, his mood has not improved over the years. Children at all grade levels studied in the same classroom, with the older children helping the younger ones. (Courtesy of Mary Bernard Silva)

Tiburon School in 1901 or 1902. The stern-looking teacher at the upper left is "Bulldog" Leeds, as the children called her. She is holding quite still, unlike most of her class, who are dressed to the nines, clutching hats, and wishing the ordeal were over.

The first Belvedere School, in the 1890's. The teacher at the top of the stairs looks bemusedly off into the middle distance. It is a charmingly natural school portrait; the boys have assumed their fiercest looks, and the girls seem unable to repress a native skepticism. (Courtesy John Meenan)

F PHOTO ENG CO

Visitors wore their Sunday best in the early 1890's on the beach at Lyford's Glen Cove (now Keil Cove). Are they prospective buyers of lots in Lyford's Hygeia? Bluff Point looms in the background.

Opposite, below: John Keefe and his family on an outing, all looking rather solemn. Keefe, who was port captain of the Corinthian Yacht Club, is credited with salvaging the social saloon of the old ship China in 1886 and converting it to a residence on Beach Road. (Courtesy Corinthian Yacht Club)

Married in 1894, Alexander McCombie and Louise Heebner settled in Tiburon. Alexander, a native of England, worked as bartender, then as a carpenter for the railroad, then as a chicken rancher in what is now Seafirth. In 1913, unable to buy land from the Reed family, the McCombies moved to a 640-acre ranch in Calaveras County. Alexander died at the age of 96 and Louise lived to be 100. (Courtesy of Grace McCombie Wolfe)

Miss Leeds, principal and teacher of grades 5-8, and Miss Dearing, who taught grades 1-4, stood on the porch with their pupils clustered all around at Tiburon School in 1906. (Courtesy of Miriam Bradley Grbac)

*The first Reed School, about 1910.
Located where Belveron West is now,
the school functioned from 1874 to
1921. Mary Bernard Silva, standing
fourth from right, donated the picture.*

*Opposite, below: The first Tiburon
School, built in 1901 and twice
replaced, seen from the lagoon in an old
postcard, about 1910. Today the
foreground is filled land, the arks are
gone, and the third school has been
converted to the Bradley House
apartments.*

*A jaunty group in varied garb, one holding a raccoon on a leash, gathered on the steps of the
Corinthian Yacht Club sometime in the 1890's. (Courtesy of the Corinthian Yacht Club)*

*This lively scene is entitled "1911 Celebration of New Clubhouse." At left, spectators cheer on their favorites as a diver neatly
enters the water. (Courtesy Corinthian Yacht Club)*

This picture seems to embody the meaning of the word
Belvedere

*A woman feeds her chickens and ducks on the lagoon in
the vicinity of San Rafael Avenue in Belvedere, 1901.
(Courtesy of Frank Wulzen)*

Dr. Florence Scott, general practioner extraordinary, is still fondly remembered by longtime residents for her trips to sickbeds on stormy nights and other missions of mercy. A graduate of the University of California Medical Department in 1896, one of eight women in a class of 52, Dr. Scott practiced in San Francisco until 1906 and then moved to Belvedere. Dr. Scott had an office in San Francisco again in the 1920's but kept her local practice. She died in 1930.

Out for a Sunday stroll about 1919, this woman found a dramatic backdrop for her picture at Lyford's Tower. Someone else is curled up against the stone wall at the entrance to the tower, perhaps hiding from the camera. (Courtesy Joseph Baird, Jr.)

The Time Cards baseball team represented NWP in 1917, when this picture was taken. They played teams from other towns and from Army posts at Angel Island and Fort Barry. The 1917 Time Cards were (standing), Jack Creighton, Jack Boche, Louie Larsen, Frank Mullin, Adolph Bergman, "Pinkie" Burns, Ray Williamson, "Bochy" Bertoli; (sitting), Ray O'Connell, Johnny Creighton, "Snoot" Wosser, Walt Griffin, manager, Billy Beyries, "Toots" McNeill, Doug Wosser, and "Bum" Beyries, mascot.

Sam Chapman, a genuine home town hero, went to Tiburon School and then to Tamalpais High, playing baseball with local teams. At Tam he was a five-letter man; at UC/Berkeley he was a football all-American. Graduating in 1934, he played with the Philadelphia Athletics, then Cleveland, and after WWII, with the Oakland Oaks, before retiring. In 1984 he was elected to the College Football Hall of Fame.

(Courtesy Pauline Zocchi)

Three tranquil scenes from three different periods. Top, 1930's; center, 1920's, right, 1984

(Philip Molten, Photographer)

Members of the eighth grade class pose with their
teacher at Tiburon School in 1929. With their
sophisticated hairdos, graceful postures, and
statuesque proportions, the girls look about four
years older than the boys.

In 1953 eighth graders of Reed School and their
teacher, Joyce Wilson, paid a visit to Lyford's
Tower, one of the subjects they were researching for
their local history, Shark Point-High Point. Note
the "For Sale" sign in the window of the tower.

The first Tiburon Fire Department (1941): August Oldag, first fire chief, is at the wheel; Ed Dunn, assistant chief, in front of him; the others are, clockwise, Arturo Scandroglio, kneeling; George Schleicher, Charles Pastori, Jr., Donald McLean, Charles Pastori, Sr., Dick Perry, Louis Soldavini, John McNeil, Guy Rhodes, C.W. Lasham, Hugo Cattani, Anthony Raberio, Bert Hooper, Mike Barnes, John Musso and Dick Williamson. (Courtesy Tiburon Fire Department) Below: Wearing "turnouts" with reflective tape, members of the 1984 Tiburon Fire Department pose with their 1973 Ward La France fire truck/at a volunteer training session: counter-clockwise, William Kehoe, (kneeling), Stephen Lynch, David Martin, Franklin Buscher, chief, Dennis Gerbich, Rodney Foster, Steven Davis, Brian Lynch, Kenneth Rogers, Lawrence Bogel, Nobou Kuwatani, Gary Lucas, Jeffery Bellinger, Richard Pearce, Mark Pearce, James Gawley, Raymond Lynch, Robert Brooks (at wheel of truck).

A panorama of downtown Tiburon taken from Corinthian Island in 1984 shows the entire site of the railroad yards, from the Tiburon Lodge at left to the old depot at far right, ready for the construction of Point Tiburon, a complex of condominiums and small shops.

The bay side of Main Street provides a fine shelter on a sunny winter day in 1984.

The massive ferry slips are gone, leaving open water all the way to Angel Island. By 1994 this picture will have begun to look quaint; in thirty years it will seem antique. With luck, the Donahue Building will still be there, more handsome than ever. (Philip Molten, photographer)

Ferry boat service to San Francisco resumed in 1962 on a modest scale. A high tide can mean wet feet for the passenger.

A highlight is the blessing of the pleasure craft, a custom originated in 1963 by Capt. Elmer Towle of the Corinthian Yacht Club. Boats sail past a Navy ship anchored offshore to hear the blessing from clergymen on board. (Philip Molten, photographer)

Boats of every description celebrate
Opening Day on the Bay the last Sunday
of April. The event is sponsored by the
Pacific Interclub Yacht Association,
comprised of yacht clubs of Northern
California. (Photo: Jocelyn Knight;
Courtesy The Ark)

Hundreds of boats, flags flying, take part in
the big parade, a treat for shorebirds as
well as sailors. (Photo: Silsby Pellissero,
Courtesy The Ark)

The flag goes up at the
Tiburon Yacht Club,
newest on the peninsula,
founded in 1969 as
Paradise Harbor Yacht
Club; the name was
changed in 1980. The
clubhouse is at
Paradise Cay.

Ring Point, a smooth, grassy hill, jutted into the Bay when this picture was taken in the 1950's. (Courtesy George Hansen)

The hill has been reorganized into fingers of land at Paradise Cay. (Philip Molten, photographer)

Strawberry changed rather suddenly from cowpasture to suburb in 1953.

Hikers enjoy Ring Mountain Preserve a few months after it was dedicated in April, 1983. This hill was slated for a massive housing development until conservationists took a stand. (Photo: Steve Cochran, Courtesy Ring Mountain Preserve)

145

The Donahue Building has seen many storms in its century on the Tiburon waterfront. (Philip Molten, photographer)

People who live at the water's edge can expect to get wet occasionally: San Rafael Avenue, December, 1983. (Photo: Diane Smith)

Sailboats, like seagulls, all face the same way. (Philip Molten, photographer)

The herring run every winter brings fishermen flocking to Elephant Rock to scoop up fish in nets. Not everything has changed in a hundred years (see pp. 31, 44).
(Philip Molten, Photographer)

This picture was taken from Mt. Tamalpais; it is undated, but was certainly taken before 1900. Mill Valley is a scattering of houses and a puff of smoke. Sausalito has its narrow-gauge railroad, but there is no visible sign of tracks or trestle in Tiburon. The whole peninsula is treeless except for Da Silva's Island, which is heavily forested. This is how the land might have looked to John Reed when he planted a cross on Mt. Tam in 1837.

This view from Belvedere was made after 1911, when the new Corinthian Yacht Club was built. The cove is so calm that the arks look as if they are suspended in air.

Some Aerial Views

Aerial views hold the same kind of interest as do old maps; one finds great pleasure in poring over them — preferably with a magnifying glass — because nothing else so clearly conveys the lay of the land and the changes that overtake it as the years pass. Some of these changes are shocking. The Tiburon Peninsula from the air resembles a chubby arm with the hand reaching toward the morsel of Angel Island; Belvedere is the thumb. The camera shows us how we butcher the land thoughtlessly in order to build a town or a railroad or a subdivision, and how as years pass the wound heals, and nature, with some help from gardeners, restores order and harmony and beauty.

The views in this section are arranged in chronological order; the first two are not strictly aerial, since they were made before airplanes. Some views are turned sideways in order to make them as large as possible.

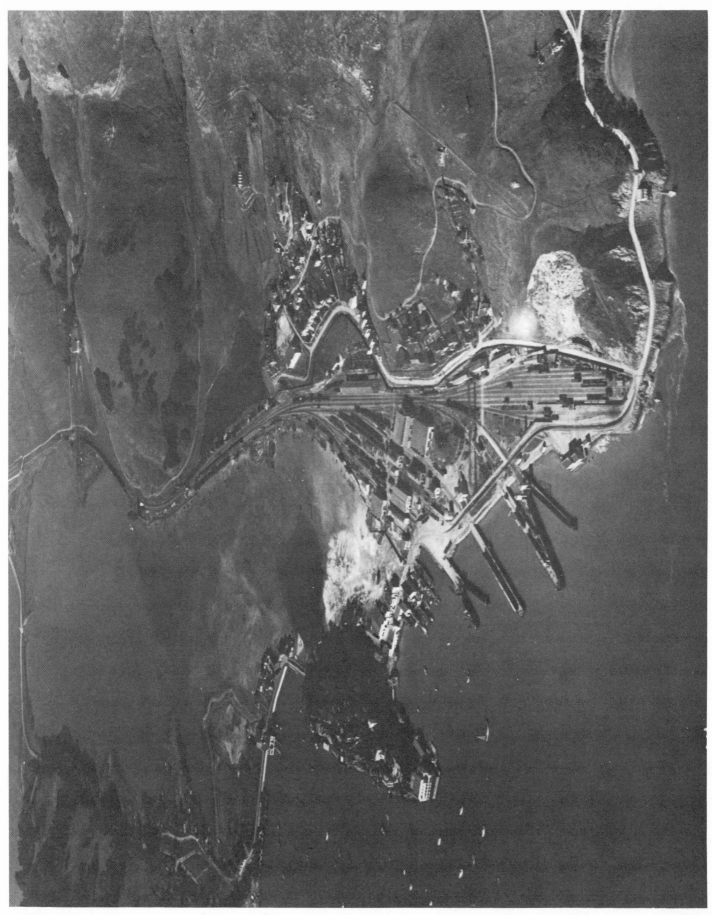

This mid-1920's view shows the old depot (top right), the roundhouse, the "new" shop with an accordian-pleated roof. The waterfront, once a few feet behind the roundhouse, has slowly advanced into the cove over the years. The shuttle ferry Marin is in her slip, just below a line of freight cars parked on a wharf. Main street still has water on both sides.

This first true aerial view (from a plane) was made in about 1926 by Waters & Hamlin Studios of Oakland. The direct highway to Tiburon has not yet been built; the only road into town is via San Rafael Avenue and Belvedere. The lagoon is still open, with a deep channel passing under the drawbridge. A daring house has sprouted on the cliff next to Lyford's Tower. The first Tiburon school has been replaced by a new building. The dairy farm at Hilarita has its own railroad station.

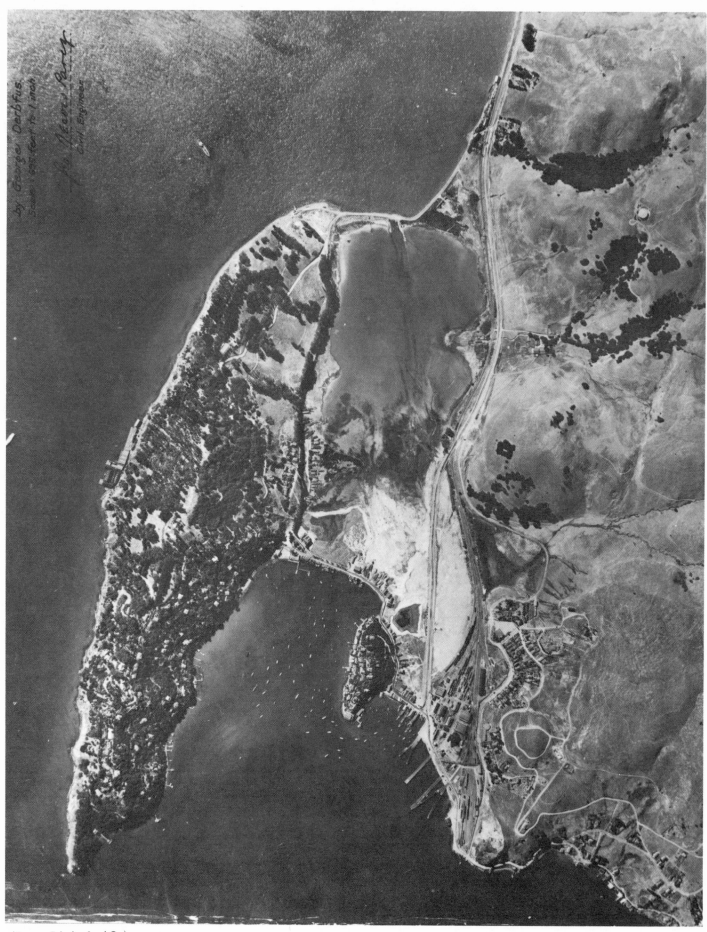

by George Derbfus.
Scale 1 695 feet to 1 inch

Jas Neare Reevy
Civil Engineer

(Courtesy Belvedere Land Co.)

Eighteen years have passed, and the battle between land and water has largely ended in a truce. The lagoon, for years a mosquito-infested mudflat, has been dredged, and the silt made into peninsulas where houses are to be built. Houses have started creeping up the hillsides above Tiburon Boulevard.

This remarkable picture was made by George Derbfus from an altitude of 16,700 feet in 1936. The lagoon, full of silt dredged from the coves, is completely shut off from the bay except for a small inlet under San Rafael Avenue. The drawbridge has been replaced by a solid structure, and the old deep channel behind today's Ark Row is only a puddle. The new highway (1929) crosses the railroad tracks to the left of Hilarita and leads straight down to Main Street, across what was open water just a few years earlier. On the west side of Belvedere the old codfishery is still in operation, with just one more year to go. The north end of Belvedere is a golf course. The arks, with no lagoon to float in, have been lined up along Corinthian Island, Beach Road, and San Rafael Avenue.

Overleaf: This very comprehensive view — it must have been a beautiful day — was made in 1953. Strawberry is suddenly home to a whole new population. There is a raw, scraped look to the new housing tracts; no trees have softened the incisions of streets. A new house and lot sold for $15,000 to $18,000. The old trestle (center left) bisects a new subdivision at Trestle Glen. Below it the railroad track emerges from its tunnel, passes the Reed Ranch, and enters another tunnel, emerging at lower left.

153

This view from 1955 shows that the railroad is still a powerful presence. Building sites on the hill above are slowly filling up. (Courtesy B.A. Lang)

Tiburon looks very tidy in 1957. Rows of cars — virtually every one made in Detroit — are nibbling at the edge of the railroad yards, and a new shopping center, the Boardwalk, is booming, with a new post office across the street. The area between the post office and Main Street is clearly in transition: anything could happen there. On the south side of Main Street is a broad new wharf, ready for occupancy. The houses on the lagoon already have a settled look. Hilarita apartments are bright white rectangles. The San Francisco Yacht Club has a new dock.

This picture shows dramatically the triumph of the automobile, virtually complete by 1965. (Philip Molten, photographer)

The long view, (1960) stretching from Stinson Beach to San Quentin, shows the
transformation of Ring Point into Paradise Cay (right). The Tiburon Peninsula is now
wholly residential; the dairy farms have completely vanished. (Courtesy Aero Photographers)

Two views of Strawberry, 1954 and 1984, show how a dairy farm was transformed into the Golden Gate Baptist Theological Seminary, with magnificent landscaping including a private forest on the round knob where an Indian village once flourished. At the tip are some of the most expensive houses ever built in Marin. The land has been tamed, and has healed its wounds.

160

Place Names: Fragments of History*

Tiburon

Tiburon — Spanish for shark, is one of Marin's oldest place names. The earliest known reference to the name is 1823, the year Father Jose Altimira noted in hs diary that he and his party stopped at *Punta del Tiburon*. As a word, *tiburon* dates back to the 15th century when Spanish explorers in the Caribbean first encountered the shark. They had no name for it, so they adopted the native Carib word, and for 400 years it has been part of the Spanish language.

Later Spanish visitors to California knew what to call sharks when they saw them. Evidently there were plenty to be seen here, since the name caught on. Shark experts say this area serves as a breeding ground for several near-shore species. A cavorting shark is featured on the Tiburon town seal.

Corinthian Island — A new yacht club was organized in 1886 and named the Corinthian, apparently taking one of the various meanings of the name, for amateur yachtsman (or perhaps "man about town, especially one who lives luxuriously or dissolutely"?) Later that year a clubhouse was built at the tip of the little island between Tiburon and Belvedere. In 1907 the Corinthian Island Co. was organized to develop the island. (Between these events, the island was sometimes called Valentine's for Thomas B. Valentine, the land speculator who owned it.) When a new clubhouse was built in 1912, it sported Corinthian columns.

Lyford's Cove — The first subdivision on the Tiburon peninsula was Lyford's Hygeia, named for a Goddess of Health. Dr. Benjamin Lyford had the area surveyed in 1883 and the southern portion was resubdivided in 1894. Most of the names survived. In his brochure Lyford explained that he gave the streets Spanish names that "had a pleasant sound and had meanings in connection with their location". Thus Vastazo (now Vistazo) Street, the highest, meant vast view; Mar Street, street by the sea; and Diviso, a dividing street. Esperanza was for hope and Reposo, for repose, later became Paradise. Connecting streets include Agreste (rustic); Linda Vista (pretty view); Loma (small hill); Solano (variant of solana, sunny place); Vista del Mar (view of the sea). Perhaps as a whim, Lyford gave two lanes double names: Paseo Walk (Walk Walk) and Vereda Path (Path Path).

Mount Tiburon — This is an old name for the 780-foot-high peak. Locally the popular name was Sugar Loaf. The original name was restored in 1962 when the subdivision was named Mount Tiburon.

Paradise Cove — Paradise is an old name used here perhaps as early as the 1860's, its origin unknown, for stretches of cove and beach on the east side of the Tiburon Peninsula.

Ring Mountain — George E. Ring, county supervisor 1895-1903, owned the California City tract below the mountain from 1879 until his death in 1913. The point of the tract jutting into the Bay came to be called Ring Point, and the mountain also acquired that name.

Waterspout Point — According to a local story, sailing ships during the Gold Rush took on water here after it was brought down from the hills through hollow logs. The name is *Linda Punta de Penascos* (Pretty Point of Rocks) on the Lyford's Hygeia map.

Belvedere

An internationally popular place name, *belvedere* is an Italian word meaning beautiful view. It dates from the first subdivision map filed by the Belvedere Land Company in 1890. Belvedere is the sixth name the island has had since the 1830's, when John Reed referred to it as *El Potrero de la Punta del Tiburon* (the Pasture of Point Tiburon). In the 1850's it was Kashow's Island, after Israel Kashow, and in 1867 the army, not wanting to take sides in a land title dispute, called it Peninsula Island. It was next Promontory Island, a name sometimes used by the army; and then, in the 19th C., Still Island.

Angel Island

This has been the name for more than 200 years. The original form was Spanish, *Isla de los Angeles* (Island of the Angels) on Lt. Juan Manuel de Ayala's 1775 chart. Some historians assert that the proper name is *Isla Santa Maria de los Angeles* (Island of Saint Mary of the Angels); others prefer *Isla de Nuestra Señora de los Angeles* (Island of Our Lady of the Angeles).

Five points of land were named by Cmdr. Cadwalader Ringgold, U.S.N., during a charting expedition in 1849: Point Blunt for Lt. Simon F. Blunt; Point Campbell for A.H. Campbell, civil engineer; Point Knox for Lt. Samuel R. Knox; Point Stuart for Frederick D. Stuart, hydrographer. Point Simpton appears on the chart but he was not identified; nor is "Ione" for whom Point Ione is named on an 1877 Army map. Quarrying (1851-1922) gave Quarry Point its name. There was a post office on Angel Island, 1875-1946.

Ayala Cove — The little Spanish vessel *San Carlos* anchored in the cove in the late summer of 1775, while her commander, Lt. de Ayala, directed the first survey of San Francisco Bay. First called Hospital Cove, it was dedicated as Ayala Cove in 1969.

Rac(c)oon Strait — The British sloop-of-war *Racoon*, careened on the beach for repairs in 1814, left her name.

Winslow Cove — China Cove, as it was called during Immigration Station days (1905-1941) was renamed in 1966 in honor of Charles A. Winslow, chairman of the Angel Island Foundation which was instrumental in gaining state park status for the island.

Strawberry Peninsula

Strawberry Point is an old name, dating from 1852 when it appeared on one of the earliest Coast Survey charts. The first surveyors needed names to refer to the various points of land; why they selected "Strawberry" for this one wasn't explained. The point was also called *Almejas* (mussels). Another name was Davis Point for Peter P. Davis, who leased the peninsula in 1864. Development of modern Strawberry began in 1947.

Richardson Bay — William Antonio Richardson was an Englishman who became the first port captain in San Francisco and built the first house there, both in 1835. Later he was granted *Rancho Sausalito*.

De Silva Island — The island derives its name from the first owner, Anthony Ferreira de Silva, who bought land in 1873. Apparently he already lived here, since on an 1869 map the name is "Pleasant Island Cap. Silvia."

* From research on Marin County place names by Louise Teather. The etymology of the name Tiburon is by courtesy of Betty Goris, Spanish Department, College of Marin.

The first Tiburon town council at its inaugural meeting, June 23, 1964. Left to right: Councilmen Leo Souza, Anne Ellinwood, Gordon Strawbridge (mayor), John S. Hoffmire (vice mayor), Fred C. Hannahs.

For the Record

Mayors of Tiburon

Gordon Strawbridge	1964
John S. Hoffmire	1966
William R. Bremer	1968
Branwell Fanning	1969
Denis T. Rice	1970
Albert Sennett	1972
Branwell Fanning	1973
Albert Aramburu	1974
George Ellman	1975
Donald Tayer	1976
E. Bruce Ross	1977
Hal Edelstein	1978
Joan Bergsund	1979
Philip Bass	1980
Kirk Hanson	1981
Dennis Rockey	1982
Gary Spratling	1983
Larry Smith	1984

City/Town Managers

Larry Rose	1964-1970
Bert Balmer	1971
Robert L. Kleinert	1973-present

Police Chiefs

Maurice D. Lafferty	1972
Michael Mannick	1975
John Bailey	1978-present

Fire Chiefs

August Oldag	1941
Ed Dunn	1946
Larry Coleman	1949
Jim Brunette	1950
Dick Williamson	1956
Jack Ismael	1956
Franklin J. Buscher	1956-present

Superintendents Reed Union School District

Albert Hutchinson	1951
Paul Stouffer	1957
Edward Pino	1962
H. Joe Edgington	1966
Robert Gaw	1969-70
Ralph Giovanniello	1971
Louis "Bill" Honig	1979
Bill Levinson	1981-present

Postmasters

Tiburon Post Office
Est. May 28, 1884

Israel Kashow, Jr.	1884
Michael O'Brien	1886
George W. Simpton	1890 (Mar. 15)
Henry O. Adam	1890 (Dec. 31)
William S. McMillan	1892
William D. Kelley	1893
Amelia Hayden	1895
Josephine F. O'Connell	1898
Flora B. Merrill	1902
John L. Carpenter	1904
Charles E. Chapman	1915
Fred Mantegani	1941
Claudine M. Anderson	1952-1956

Belvedere Post Office
Est. June 4, 1897

Henry C. Buhrmeister	1897
William P. Archibald	1901
Nathan E. Bishop	1904
Flora M. Winsor	1907
Elizabeth C. Ballard	1909
Sophia C. Livesey	1910
Stella Ehrenfelt	1937-1956

Blevedere-Tiburon Post Office
Consolidated June 1, 1956

Stella Ehrenfelt	1956
Theodore J. Lehman	1964
Mario H. Pompei, Jr.	1971-present

Public Parks

Angel Island State Park
Paradise Beach County Park
Tiburon Uplands Nature Preserve (County)
Town of Tiburon
  Richardson Bay Lineal Park
    Richardson Bay Path
    McKegney Green
    South of the Knoll
    Blackie's Pasture
  Belveron Park
  Allan Thompson Walkway
  Open space: 166 acres
City of Belvedere
  Harry B. Allen Park
  Lagoon Road Park
Strawberry Recreation District
  Recreation Center
  Brickyard Park
  Strawberry Cove Park
  Paths
    Belloc Lagoon
    Greenwood Bay
    Sanderling
  Open space: 5 acres; tidelands 22 acres

Index

Sponsors

A

Tane R. Abbott
Richard and Chita Abbott
Dr. & Mrs. Alan L. Abrams
William Regnar Adams
Sebastien Agajan
Donald & Bonnie Agins
Nancy & Robert Agnew
Arthur & Violet Ahlquist
Daniel & Barbara Airola
David & Irmine Airola
Jean & Lowell Airola
Jonathan & Sandra Airola
Leslie Airola
Herman & Juanita Albachten
Albatross II Book Shop
Mr. & Mrs. James C. Albert
Albertini Family
Mr. & Mrs. E. E. Albright
Michael Alderucci
Verne Alexander
Mr. & Mrs. Whitman K. Alger
Thamir & Ardath Al'Hashimi
Bruce Allan
Armand & Nancy Allegra
Ann & Howard B. Allen
Bettye B. Allen
David W. Allen
James & Nan Allen
Kent & Paola Allen
Paula & Andrew Allen
Mr. & Mrs. Robert M. Allen
Mr. & Mrs. Harry P. Altick
Anthony Ridley Amos
Leslie Bergsund Amsberry
Andy & Kathy Anderson
Bill & Nina Anderson
Bill & Posie Anderson
Dan & Carol Anderson
Mr. & Mrs. Eugene R. Anderson
John & Lindsay Anderson
Paul & Billie Anderson
Mr. & Mrs. Richard D. Anderson
Peter & Christian Andresen
Richard Andrews
Al & Yami Anolik
Beryl & Trevor Anstey
Rosemary Antonucci
Berta & Richard Appel
Helen & Fred Applegate
Paul & Linda Ardleigh
Mrs. Alfred Arnaud
Terry & Mike Arnaud
Linda Arnold
Peter & Patricia Arrigoni
Dr. & Mrs. John W. Ashford
Mrs. Raymond Aspesi
Mr. & Mrs. William A. Atchley, Jr.
Mr. & Mrs. Robert W. Atkinson
Jaclyn Attabit
Kirby Ann Atterbury
Marianne & Charles Auerbach
Carol Augustus
Leona & JoAnn Avery

B

Jack & Eleanor Babat
Elly Babat's Drama School
Paula Law Bacciocco
Howard & Shirley Backen

Mr. & Mrs. Richard C. Bacon
Mr. & Mrs. Jan Baden
Mr. & Mrs. Donald T. Baird
Dr. Joseph A. Baird, Jr.
Cam & Kate Baker
Mr. Hank Baker
Jim & Julie Baker
North Baker
Molly Bakkum
Stephanie Rice Ballachey
David & Shirley Ballash
Herbert & Marianne Bals
Kathryn Stockfleth Barcos
Marjorie Barling
Richard & Jennifer Barker
David & Airdrie Barley
Per & Veslemoy Barnes
Roma Barnes & children
Lester & Judith Barnett
Jim & Jean Barnett
Nancy J. Bartusch
Philip & Sharon Bass
Mr. & Mrs. Edward C. Bassett
Joan L. Bassett
Ann V. Bastian
James A. Bastian
Mr. & Mrs. Richard J. Bates
Donald L. Batten
Mary & Frank Baumgarten
Norman & Caprice Bautista
Irene & Genevieve Bayreuther
Laurie Beacock
Max & Claudia Beagarie
Ronald A. Becker
Jack J. Beckerman
Loretta, Beckman-Carr
Diane Beeston
Peter & Drago Bego
Ruth & Tom Behrens
Stan & Nancy Behrens
Roland & Anne Beisenstein
Joan & Don Bekins
Bel Aire School
Charles & Helena Bell
Dr. & Mrs. Russell Bell
Adam Stone Bellinger
Travis Armstrong Bellinger
Belvedere - Tiburon Branch Library
Helen & Howard Benedict
Glidden Ross Benefield
Leslie & Carol Benet
Diana & Michael Bennett
Dave & Ann Benoit
Hatsy & Cliff Benton
Alexis Ross Berger
Miles & Piper Berger
Joan & Richard Bergsund
Richard Leif Bergsund
Sara Gail Bergsund
Anita & Frederick Berman
Jerome J. Bernal
William & Christine Berry
Dr. & Mrs. Carroll H. Berryman
Mimi & George C. Berticevich
Mario Bertolucci
Patricia R. Bertrand
Carolee & David Bessie
Mr. & Mrs. Paul Beuttas
Hakan & Mona Bille
Gordon Bird
Caroline & Brandon Birich

Mr. & Mrs. John A. Bischoff
Mrs. R. J. Bishop
Douglas, Black
Dorothy S. Blackmore
Mr. & Mrs. Ralph E. Blair
Helen Blanchard
Blasdell Family
Peggy & David Blatchford
Bernard & Linda Blatte
Bill & Tamera Blogg
Mr. & Mrs. Emanuel Bloom
Henry P. Bode
Mr. & Mrs. Richard E. Boesel
Larry & Barbara Bogel
Stephen & Lydia Bogel
Walter & Bea Bogel
Mr. & Mrs. Logan Boles
Patricia Bosqui
Sarane T. Bowen
Mark Patrick Bowen
William M. Bowen
Dione & Stewart Bowers
Mrs. Avis Boyden
W. E. Boyer
Fay Boyle
Syd Boyle
David & Diane Bradford
Clay & Diana Bradley
Mr. Frank W. Brady
Mr. & Mrs Martin Bramante
Dr. & Mrs. Robert Branick
William T. Brantman
Tracy Brash
Bill & Peggy Bremer
Billy Bremer
Karen Bremer
Mark Bremer
Mr. Bob Brewer
David & Sandra Brewer
Jules Bricken
Violet Collins Bricker
Mrs. Arthur F. Bridge
Jack & Nancy Bridges
Wade & Connie Brightbill
Henry J. & Mary Jo Broderick
Mrs. John Brooke
Pat & Frank Brooks
Daniel Steven Brown
Kenneth Scott Brown
Mrs. Mary Grace Brown
Thomas & Anne Brown
Mr. & Mrs. Charles Browne
Hank Bruce
Louis F. & Virginia R. Brunini
Walther & Wendy Buchen
Pat & Gene Buck
Carol Connelly Budds
E. Rick Buell II
William James Buell
Mary Lu Buich
Mr. & Mrs. Ray Bunker
Bradford & Bruce Bunnell
Charmaine A. Burdell
Gene & Sammie Burke
William & Rosalie Burket
Brian & Bonnie Burns
Frederick R. Burrell
Frank & Eileen Burrous
Stuart D. Burt
Ms. Carol Burton
Robert E. Burton

Franklin & Maureen Buscher
Fred & Barbara Buscher
Fred J. Buscher
Eva Buxton

C

Mr. & Mrs. Wm. D. Caddell
Mr. & Mrs. Gerald Cahill
Mrs. John E. Cahill
California Health Research Foundation
Dr. & Mrs. Enoch Callaway
Charles Warren Callister
Callister, Gately & Bischoff
Mary Frances Callister
Mr. Glen Calkins
Roy & William Cameron
Anne & Tony Campodonico
Alice Cannistraci
Angelo & Louise Capozzi
Robert & Nancy Cappelloni
The Caprice Restaurant
Susan & Richard Card
Mr. & Mrs. A. Cariani
Mr. & Mrs. Burlington Carlisle
Marilyn Ann Carlson
Jeanette & Martin Carr
Keith Carr
Patricia I. Carranza
Barbara Sesnon Cartan
Hazel & Gary Carter
William & Dorothy Carter
James & Mavis Caruso
George & Mary Lee Casey
Joseph & Marlene Casey
Gandolf Catagin
Mrs. Hugo Cattani
Mr. & Mrs. Garry Cecil
Adrienne & Milton Cerf
Mr. & Mrs. Richard Cerutti
Mr. & Mrs Kenneth L. Chamberlain
Lowell & Patsy Chamberlain
Bill and O'Hara Chapin
Bryan & Jenny Chapman
Arthur Munro Christian
Belle Clapper
Barbara & Richard Clark
Darrell & Kay Clark
Derrith Richter Clark
James Weart Clark
Don Clauder
Dr. & Mrs. Francis J. Clauss
Brad & Debbie Cleland
Dr. & Mrs. John A. Clements
Donald & Kathleen Cliggett
Henri & Vera Clouette
Minna & Bill Clum
Margaret LaPlace Coates
Fred Codoni
Jean & Mel Cohen
Mr. & Mrs. Stanton E. Colbert
Bonnie Jean Cole
Mr. & Mrs. Herbert A. Cole
Mervyn & Anna-Jean Cole
Mr. & Mrs. Ralph N. Cole
George & Mollie Coleman
John H. Coleman
Lawrence & Audrey Coleman
Jerry Coletta
James Farish Collbran
Mr. & Mrs. Joseph S. Colletto
Mr. & Mrs. William W. Collier
Jean M. Colton
Laurence A. Colton
Mr. & Mrs. John Colver

Mr. & Mrs. R. N. Congreve
Dolores & George Conlan
Mr. George B. Conlan
Dr. & Mrs. Robert H. Conner
Dr. & Mrs. Peter A. Conroy
Mrs. John W. Converse
Daniel & Alice Cook
Nancy Cook
Ray & Judy Coombes
Dr. & Mrs. Patrick Coonan
Mr. & Mrs. Allen Cooper
Dave Cooper
Harry & Harriet Cooper
Mr. & Mrs. Jack R. Cooper
Michael & Helen Cooper
Elizabeth & Fulton Copp
Hart W. Corbett
Corinthian Yacht Club
Alfred Corn
Peter Corn
Polly Corn
Sallie Corn
Samual Corn
Mrs. Thomas L. Corn
William & Adele Corvin
Jan Gregg Coughlan
James V. Coulter
Jack Courtney
Suzanne & Eric Cowing
E. Morris Cox
Winifred & William Cox
Stone & Suzanna Coxhead
Dr. & Mrs. Thomas Cromwell
Mr. & Mrs. Joseph Cronin
Mr. & Mrs. Robert Crowder
Thomas B. Crowley
John & Mary Croxall
Ann L. Cruchley
Crunelle Family
Mrs. Vivian O. Cummings
Alan & Anne Cundall
Mrs. J. R. Cunningham
G. & K. Curincione-Coles
Dave & Carol H. Curtis
John S. & Evelyn M. Curtis
Arthur Cushing, Esq.
Mr. & Mrs. Edward Cutter

D

Chuck & Joan Dahlgren
Bo & Catherine Dahlstrom
Robin Snow Daly
Mr. & Mrs. Vernon Dallman
Tom & Barbara Dandurand
Charles & Esther Daniels
Carl F. Danielson
Steve & Dorothy Darden
Janet & Sid Daru
Mr. & Mrs. F. B. Davidson
Don & Lee Davis
Mr. & Mrs. Donald G. Davis
James & Christine Davis
Ken & Ann Davis
Mr. & Mrs. Peter A. Davis
Shantala & Jayger Davis
Steven N. Davis
Mr. & Mrs. John Dawson
Defenderfer Family
Mr. & Mrs. Thomas Deffebach
D. Gail & John DeLalla
Charles Deleuze
Del Mar School
Thomas & June DeVille
Ann & Elmo L. De Martini

Loring A. & Francine De Martini
B. G. Deming
Dr. & Mrs. Norman J. DeMont
Helene & Jim Denebeim
Mr. & Mrs. Thomas E. Denson
Jerome T. & Nancy H. Denz
Dr. & Mrs. Richard Derby, Jr.
Barbara Fanning Derkacht
Thomas & Anita Desimini
Aldo & Elizabeth de Tomasi
William & Sarah Devlin
Mr. & Mrs. R. James Diepenbrock
Terry Lyons Di Gangi
Bonnie & Bernie Dignam
Terry Meyers Dillingham
Clare E. Dimmock
Betty E. Dippel
David Michael Dolson
Joan & Hillary Don
Mr. & Mrs. David Donzel
John & Lyn Dooley
Craig & Jill Dorsey
Jay & Patsy Doty
Caren Atterbury Dougherty
Margaret Wosser Dowd
Alison M. Dowse
Maxwell & Jan Drever
Larry & Ann Drew
Fred & Jane Drexler
Josephine C. Duff
William Robert Duff
Mr. & Mrs. Franklin Dumm
William E. Dunlap, Jr.
Mr. Peter Dunn
David J. Dupont
Scott Joseph Dupont
Thomas A Dupont, Jr.
Mr. & Mrs. Fred Dupuis
Susan Dupuis
Durney Bros.
Charles and Sallie Durrie

E

Fred & Doris Eberts
Sylvia Eberts-Silewicz
Hal & Claire Edelstein
Thomas & Mary Edmiston
Jeff & Donna Egeberg
Mr. & Mrs. Robert D. Egner
Alan & Jean Ehrenberg
Stella A. Ehrenfelt
Philip & Sheila Ehrlich
Jean Casey Eichelberger
Erling Eide
Rolf Eiselin
Mr. & Mrs. David Eklund
Mr. & Mrs. Gerald J. Elbert
Janet & Rex Elder
Orchid M. & Roy E. Eldred
Theodore L. & Martha B. Eliot
Anne L. Ellinwood
George & Phyllis Ellman
Caroline Croci Elliott
Robert James Elliott
Rita Ellis
Mrs. Nina Eloesser
Robert & Cynthia Elsberg
Jeanne Meyers Embry
Ragnar & Sally Engebretsen
Bill & Susan Englebright
Lars & Marion Engstrom
Jim & Marie Enzensperger
Environmental History
Helen Symes Epperson

Mr. & Mrs. Arnold Epstein
Drs. Charles J. & Lois B. Epstein
John & Carol C. Ericson
Erik & Joan Erikson
Dan & Lynette Erlach
Robert & Edna Erwin
Shirley & Randolph Esplin
David & Carol Essick
Mr. Michael & Dr. Jacqueline Etemad
Ann & Bob Evans
Harriet & David Evans
Mr. & Mrs. Darrel Ewing
Reuben & Freda Ewing

F

Faggioli Family
Dr. & Mrs. H. Barrie Fairley
Baldhard & Mary Falk
Branwell & Carolyn Fanning
Mr. & Mrs. Ben Farlatti
Artelle & Erwin Farley
Jack A. Farley
John Farley
Leon & Patricia Farley
Mr. Johann Farmont
Mary & Perrin Fay
Ellen & Peter Feinman
Ms. Margy Felcher
Gregory Ross Felton
Louise Felton
Marcia & Roger Felton
Timothy Mattox Felton
David & Julie Fenix
Lucy & Jack Fenstermaker
Alan & Priscilla Fenton
Fifty-five Main Street Investors
M. B. Figari
Dorothy Figour
Charles & Erin Findlay
R. H. Fink
John Finn III
Mr. Bill Finsterbush
First Nationwide Savings
Mr. & Mrs. A. Robert Fisher
Michael & Carolyn Fitz-Gerald
Ralph & Judy Fleming
Mr. & Mrs. John O. Flender
Dr. & Mrs. John H. Flint
Patricia K. & Andrew C. Fluegelman
David & Carol Fluke
Howard & Erdmuth Folker
Patricia J. Fonarow
Dr. & Mrs. Barry L. Fong
Bill Foote
Ron Foote
Sandra Foote
Mr. & Mrs. Chris Ford
Nicholas & Carol Forell
C. H. Ned Forrest
John E. Fortanas
Mr. Lewis P. Foster
Mr. Lewis P. Foster, Jr.
Lynne Frances Foster
Marshall & Joan Foster
Carole & Alexander Fox
Robert A. & Susan D. Fox
Mrs. Elmer Fraass
Mary L. Franck
Susan C. Franck
Nancy Bickelhaupt Frank
Kay & Jack Freckmann
Ruth & Roy Freeburg
Roger & Nancy Freed
Michael Friedman

Michelle & Robert Friend
Lynne & Evelyn Frisbee
Linda Fritschner
Gisela & Max Fritz-Graefe
Donald & Patricia L. Furlong
Ralph & Donna Funicello
Thomas J. Furner, Jr.
Victors R. Furst Family
Helen P. Furtado

G

Verl & Ruth Gale
Frank & Jean Galli
Jerry Ganz
Andy & Brigitta Garde
Mr. & Mrs. Duane B. Garrett
Dana Garrick
Melissa Garrick
Dr. & Mrs. Richard Garrick
Herb & Annette Gaskin
Dr. & Mrs. James M. Gawley
Christina Gazulis
Dr. & Mrs. James P. Geiger
Fred & Annette Gellert
Mr. & Mrs. George R. Geppert
Mahmoud Ghazanfarpour
Claire B. Gilbert
David & Cynthia Gilbert
Donald L. & Marjory B. Gilbert
Jeanette & Alexandra Gilbert
Law Offices of Cynthia Gilbert, Inc.
Thomas William Gille
Mr. Richard F. Gilman
Ivan & Bruna Ginesi
Mr. & Mrs. Everett A. Girtler
john & Gertrude Giuliani
Mr. & Mrs. John Gleason
Mr. & Mrs. Richard Gledhill
Barbara & George Gnoss
John & Ruth Gobershock
Mr. & Mrs. Geoff Goddard
George & Sheret Goddard
Marc & Gregory Goldberg
Elaine W. Gordon
Mr. & Mrs. Laverne E. Gordon
Marty Gordon
Mr. & Mrs Ralph T. Gordon
Daniel F. Gould Co., Inc.
Frances H. Gould
Leslie & Alice Graham
Tom & Janice Gram
Charles R. Grant
Ruth & Rollin Grant
Mrs. John Graves III
Miriam Bradley Grbac
Mr. & Mrs. Robert Greber
Dr. & Mrs. Richard M. Greenberg
Gary & Fredrica Greene
Mr. & Mrs. Richard L. Greene
Drs. John & Deborah Greenspan
Nicholas & Louise Greenspan
Mr. & Mrs. Jack Grey
Robert & Judy Gries
Jack & Shirley Griffin
Melbourne E. Griffin
Sara G. & Richard M Griffith, Jr.
Robert & Nannette Griswold
William T. & Leonie Griswold
David & Ellie Gross
Marshall & Shelby Gross
Rosemary Grow
Arthur Groza
Elvira & Pat Guagliano
Sandra Lynn Guaglianone

Gerald P. Guerin, Sr.
Robert & Nancy Guider
Mr. & Mrs. A. M. Guzzardo
Michael A. Guzzardo

H

Mr. & Mrs. George Hackworth
Robert & Vivian Hadley
James Hahn
Dr. & Mrs. Richard S. Hahn
David H. Haines
David W. Hall
Knowles L. & Sherry A. Hall
Wallace & Elizabeth Hall
Mr. & Mrs. Brooke Powell Halsey, Sr.
Dr. & Mrs. William T. Halsey
Mr. & Mrs. Richard B. Ham
Amy T. Hambrecht
Elizabeth Hambrecht
George N. Hambrecht
Robert M. Hambrecht
Susan Hambrecht
Mr. & Mrs. William R. Hambrecht
Jack & Mary Lou Hamilton
Ruthe Hamm
James & Sharon Hampton
Mr. & Mrs. Raymond G. Handley
Mary Burrell Hanks
Hansen Associates
Gary & Fani Hansen
Mr. & Mrs. C. S. Hanson
David S. Hanson
Kirk & Kerstin Hanson
Scott & Judy Hanson
Mr. & Mrs. George H. Harlan
Mr. & Mrs. John Harper
John & Jeanette Harrington
Alvin & Barbara Harris
John & Angela Harris
Robert L. Harrison
Bob & Pam Harryman
Charlie & Margaret Harryman
Carolyn Grant Hart
Philip C. & Nena P. Hart
Mr. & Mrs. Robert C. Harter
Dexter & Emmy Hartke
Regina & Roger Hartley
Dr. Chris Hatcher
Licia Hayden
Jeffrey Haynes
Mr. & Mrs. Lee B. Hausam
Timothy D. Hayes
Paul & Ann-Eve Hazen
Ketty & Russ Heacox
F. Cleveland & Rosalie Hedrick
Helen & Laurence Heimerl
Ernest & Doris Held
Phyllis Helfand
Emily E. Heller
H. Robert Heller
Barbara Ann Helms
Ronald J. Helow
Mr. & Mrs. Dana De Voto Hemberger
Dione & David Hemberger
Mr. & Mrs. Elmer F. Hemberger
Charles & George Henderson
Dr. & Mrs. Simon Henderson
Robert Gaston Herbert, Jr.
Dr. & Mrs. William Heydorn
Rich & Connie Hildahl
Dick & Jill Hill
Mr. & Mrs. Vaughan C. Hill
Jane & Catherine Hills
Jack Hillmer

Dr. & Mrs. Corwin Hinshaw
Mr. & Mrs. Ben B. Hirsch
E. Stanley Hobbs, Jr.
Col. & Mrs. Gregory J. Hobbs
Hal & Edith Hobbs
Mr. & Mrs. Richard L. Hobbs
Hope Hodge
Douglas Paul Hodgdon
John & Kay Hoefer
Bill & Susan Hoehler
John & Jean Hoffmire
Mr. & Mrs. John R. Hofmann Jr.
Florence & William Holcombe
Bernard Hollander
Virgil & Marjory Hollis
Dorothy Holmes
Graham & Maureen Holmes
Mercedes Truman Holtz
Mr. & Mrs. Chas. Homer
I'Lee & Tony Hooker
Jack & Mayvis Hooley
Mr. & Mrs. Dale E. Hopkins
Guy & Joy Hopkins
Mr. & Mrs. John W. Hopkins
Stewart & Eleanore Hopkins
Karl D. Hoppe
Carolyn Horan
William & Joanne Horton
Leo & Carlma Houweling
Mrs. Geraardt M. Howard
Mr. & Mrs Colby Howe
Ken & Jann Howie
Mr. Jules A. Hoyt
David & Robin Hudnut
Jancie & Kent Hughes
Mr. Charles V. Hulick
Mr. & Mrs. Charles V. Hulick, Jr.
Jean & Paul Hull
Gerda & Robert Humphreys
Daniel Hunt
John Brockway Huntington
Robert Huston
Karen & Richard Hyde
Molly Keil Hynes

I

David & Barbara Imrie
Martha Ireland
Mr. David Irmer
Mr. & Mrs. E. Glenn Isaacson
Mrs. Jesse J. Iverson
Ted Iverson

J

Harry & Margaret Jackson
Derek Jacobson
Henry Jacobson
James Jacobson
Jean & Berton Jacobson
Doug James
Jim & Pat James
Laurie James
Mr. & Mrs. Theodore E. James, Jr.
Dr. & Mrs. Arthur Jampolsky
Wing & Bud Jeneski
Jason Jennings
Rupert L. Jernigan
David & Violet Jesberg
Dr. & Mrs. Hartwell Jewell
Parvin & Khosro Jobrani
Mr. & Mrs. Leland M. Johns

Mr. & Mrs. Andrew Johnson
Edgar R. Johnson
Rev. George E. Johnson
Hiram W. Johnson 3rd
Joel & Pamela Johnson
Joseph A. Johnson
Keith Johnson
Mr. & Mrs. Kenneth G. Johnson
Rudin M. Johnson, Jr.
W. Burbeck & Eleanor H. Johnson
Agnes H. Johnston
Mary & Bill Johnstone
Gay Jolissaint
Bill & Adele Jonas
Barbara & Wally Jones
Mr. & Mrs. Geoffrey R. Jones
Grant & Joyce Jones
Mr. & Mrs. Milbrey Jones
Bill & Jane Joost
Julian & Susan Jourard
Charlotte Jurs
Pam Juvonen

K

Richard & Clarita Kaapuni
Mrs. Edgar M. Kahn
Louis Kahn & Family
Paul & Gerrie Kahn
Raymond Kaliski
Max & Lila C. Kalm
Saburo & Joyce Kami
Jack & Gee Kampmeyer
Alan & Audrey Kane
Donald & Joan Kane
Timothy Kane
Dr. & Mrs. Richard Kanter
Mr. & Mrs. Marc Kapellas
Jay & Dale Kaplan
Anders & Brigitta Karlman
Mr. & Mrs. Mark O. Kasanin
Mr. Frank Kawalkowski
Mr. & Mrs. Casey A. Kawamoto
Diane Keaton
Francis V. Keesling, Jr.
Mr. & Mrs. Russell D. Keil
Mr. & Mrs. Russell Keil, Jr.
Joe & Joy Keller
Michael W. & Helene L. Keller
Dr. & Mrs. C. Franklin Kelley
Dorothy P. Kelly
Patsy M. Kelly
Sallie Bell Kelly
James & Nancy Kelso
Bob & Dawn Kennedy
Elizabeth & Allan Kennedy
Constance Atterbury Kepler
Helene & Michael Keran
George & Jane Kerrigan
Scott G. Kew
Dr. & Mrs. Jules Key
Mr. & Mrs. John Kieser
Leo & Dorothy Killion
Dave & Mary Lou Kilmer
Mr. & Mrs William R. Kimball
Mrs. Yvonne Kimball
Dan & Mary J. King
Mr. & Mrs. Daniel W. King
Mr. & Mrs. Robert Norman King
Frank G. & Ruth P. King
Mr. & Mrs. John H. King
Mrs. John Lord King
Paul Barker Kingston
Charles & Lucille Kircher

David Kircher
Mr. & Mrs. Thomas Kircher
Kircher Family
Hampton & Georgia Kirchmaier
Gisela Klein
Kleinert Family
Donna & Sylvan Kline
Phyllis & Bob Knapp
Bill & Janette Knick
Geoffrey Gerara Knight
Jeff & Marilyn Knight
Jocelyn Marie Knight
William Knorp
Marion S. Knowles
Dr. & Mrs. Herbert Konkoff
Lisa Konkoff
Stephen Konkoff
Mr. & Mrs. Emanuel Z. Kopstein
Kosciusko, Ron & Shirley
Donald L. Koski
Erland T. & Lillian M. Koski
Ted & Susan Kreines
Joan Krivda
Suzanne Duffy Kuratek

L

Ira B. Laby
Mr. & Mrs. Thomas C. Lacey
Mr. & Mrs. Thomas M. Lacey
Wendy & Cal LaLanne
Babe Lamerdin
Nikki Lamott
Mr. & Mrs. Hunter Land
Patricia & Michael Land
Camille Landau
Florence Landau
George & Babette Landau
Julien Landau
Elaine Lang
Mrs. Mary J. Lang
Mr. & Mrs F. C. Lange
John & Trudy Lanser
Brian F. & Carla Lantier
Rob & Joy Lanyon
Mr. & Mrs. Henry E. Lapkin
Mr. & Mrs. Henry E. Lapkin, Jr.
Fred & Shirley Larkins
Mr. & Mrs. Kell Bredsig Larsen
Jim & Leslie La Torre
Mr. & Mrs. Charles J. Lause
Kelly, Lavik
Richard & Carolyn Lawson
Ed & Christopher Le Clair
L. M. Legac
David & Sally Legge
Charles T. Lehman
Jane Bagley Lehman
Susan Reynolds Lehman
James & Linda S. Lekas
Mr. Ted Lemen
Dr. & Mrs. Richard Leonards
Mr. & Mrs. Albert J. Lettrich
Robert & Una Levine
Bill & Judy Levinson
Mimi & Walter Levison
Walter & Enid Levison
Carson Levit
Sherry & Victor Levit
Vicky Levit
Emily & James Levorsen
Carl T. & Carol A. Lewis
Rev. & Mrs. Jack R. Lewis
Katherine Lewis

MacBoyle & Fran Lewis
Mr. Robert F. Lewitt
Mr. Greg Linde
Ronald E. Lindemann
Mrs. Charles Lindsay
Earl & Arthulene Linman
Michael & Julia Linwood
Richard & Diane Lion
John & Sandra Lisanti
Mrs. Ruth E. Lisle
Sherman & DeLaine Little
David & Hilary Llewelyn
Mr. Theodore H. Long
Mary Ellen Longstreth
Joshua & Stephanie Lonn
Don Loomis
Loraine G. Lougee
Mrs. Joan Loughlin
Peter & Patricia Love
Dr. & Mrs. Craig Lubbock
Gary & Camerin Lucas
Ken & Joan Lucas
Ola & Danica Lundberg
William & Susan Lukens
Edward & Thelma Lybrand
Alexis Rice Lydecker
John J. Lynch
Leslie & Diane Lynch
Ray & Kim Lynch
Raymond & Lois Lynch
Steph Lynch
Mr. & Mrs. Donald Lyon
Patricia & Michael Lyon

M

Leigh Allan Maca
Alfred MacAdam
Mr. & Mrs. Richard MacFarlane
Bruce MacGowan
Peter MacGowan
Mr. & Mrs. Wallace MacGregor
Mrs. Claude Mackenzie
Ken & Sherry Mackey
Kate Meyers MacKinnon
Joyce A. MacLaury
Margaret Christensen MacLaury
Margerie R. MacLaury
Richard E. MacLaury
Robert E. MacLaury
Sally S. Magneson
Melanie & Peter Maier
Mr. & Mrs. Howard Mailliard
Hon. William S. Mailliard
Mr. & Mrs. William A. Main
Victor Mainini, Jr.
Dr. & Mrs. Bruce S. Manheim
Bea & Sam Mann
Donald & Jayne Mann
Karen & Philip Mann
Mr. & Mrs. Richard Mannila
C.Edward Mannion
Mike & Gloria Mansfield
Fred & Ruth Mantegani
Mr. & Mrs. George Mantegani
Gene & Nathaniel Marans
Robert R. & Beverly L. Marcus
Warren M. Marcus
Anthony Joseph Marelich
Mr. & Mrs. Scott F. Maricle
Marin County Historical Society
Marin County Library, Calif. Room
Mr. & Mrs. Marc L. Marker
Raymond & Ruth Marks
Mr. & Mrs. G. T. Marsh

Marilyn Marsh
Bob & Penny Marshall
Griffith O. Marshall
Carl L. Martin Family
Mr. Jay R. Martin
Mary & Ralph Martindale
Allan & Eleanor Martini
Mr. & Mrs. Robert J. Martini
Ann Kelso Martinis
James B. Martinoni
Bente & Arne Martinsen
Lincoln Edward Marx
Beverly J. Mason
Mr. & Mrs. Peter A. Mason
Mr. Michael Masterson
John Matarangas
Brian Richard Matas
Cdr. Fred I. Mather
Mr. & Mrs. Santiago Matheus
Harry & Ann Mathews
Joseph & Katherine Mathews
Larry & Jan Mathews
Dr. Peter & Leslie Mathews
Lucinda M. Mathis
Mark L. Mathis
George S. May
Margaret Carroll May
Mr. & Mrs. Robert G. Mayberry
Scott & Katie Maze
Bruce & Muriel McAllister
Miss Margaret A. McAllister
Dr. & Mrs. Richard McAuliffe
Michael & Ruth McBride
Dan & Carole McCaskill
Bruce & Gwen McCauley
Aline & Frank McClain
Tim McClain
James & Susan McClatchy
Richard & Benita McConnell
Deborah & James McCray
Bob & Madeline McCrea
Kenneth McCready
Mrs. Linda B. & Curtis B. McCready
Mari McCrohan
Ray & Mary McDevitt
Milton & Mary Jane McDonogh
Pete McFarland
Ronald McFarland
Ed & Joan McFetridge
Dr. & Mrs. Joseph L. McGerity
Michael P. & Judith C. McGovern
James & Eileen McGowan
Mr. & Mrs. Patrick B. McGrath
Terry Pritchett McGuinness
Ellen Bastian McHenry
The McIlroy Family
Margaret & Malcolm McIlroy
Jack & Florence McIntyre
Mr. Ron McIntyre
Dan & Patricia McKee
Betty McKegney
W. Conrad & Loulette McKelvey
Patricia & Andrew A. McKenna
Bill & Genny McLean
Terence V. McLoughlin
Douglas & Brenda McVay
Franz McVay
Henry & Deborah McWhinney
Dr. Ann-Marie Meager & Daniel
Dr. & Mrs. Andrew M. Mecca
Kate & Andy Mecca
S. A. Megeath III
Maureen Meikle
John & Stephanie Mendel

Colin & Rae Menzies
Mr. & Mrs. William E. Mercer
Mr. & Mrs. Kenneth Merklin
Mr. & Mrs. John O. Merrill
Mr. & Mrs. Richard Mesker
Meredith & Dorothy Messer
John & K. J. Metcalf
Mr. & Mrs. Kenneth C. Metzger
Mary Stoddard Meyer
Ralph & Beverly Meyers
Mr. & Mrs. Bahman Meykadeh
Dr. & Mrs. T. S. Meyler
James & Marjorie Michael
Mr. & Mrs. William F. Michaud
Mill Valley Public Library
Mill Valley Historical Society
Robert & Christine Miller
Alan & Marlene Minkin
Sherry & Bob Minton
Louise M. Mirata
Allan & Shirley Mitchell
Vera Moitoza
Mr. & Mrs. Robert P. Molten
Sally & Allan Moltzen
Alan Mooers
Jim & Donna Moore
Mr. & Mrs. Richard J. Moore
William & Eve Moore
Jeffrey Moreau
Chris & Ewa Morgan
Dorothy & James Morgan
Gary & Dennis Morgan
Jean & Tim Morgan
Martha H. Morgan
Christopher Morrison
Keith Morrison
Mr. & Mrs. R. Edward Morrison
Mr. & Mrs. John M. Morson
Frank & Dee Moss
Josephine L. Moss
Nettie R. Mossoni
Mr. & Mrs. Robert Mott
Mount Tamalpais Primary School
Mr. & Mrs. Masoud Mousavizadeh
Mr. & Mrs. Dutch Mucklow
Joan A. Mueller
John & Brigitte Muenster
Chris & Sheila Mulvaney
Grif & Jacklyn Mumford
Lee & Beverly Munson
John & Judy Munter
Masahiro & Yasuko Murata
Dick & Jayne Murdock
Rolph & Lillian Murk
Barbara & Roy Murphy
Catherine U. Murray
D. B. & Nancy Murray
James Murray
Joseph D. & Martha M. Murray
Lesley Largman Murray
Pamela Murray
Robert & Alison Murray
John M. Mussey
John Musso
Bill & Gloria Myers
Bill & Mary Myers
Greg Myers
David F. Myrick

N

Mr. Alan Nadritch
Paul & Terry Nargiz
Mrs. Edward Naughton
Norma & Charles Neal

Cheryl Ann Neerhout
Mr. & Mrs. Eugene A. Nelson, Jr.
Marilyn & Kenneth Nemzer
Edward H. Nervo
Robert & Donna Neuerburg
Catharine Atterbury Newbury
Robert & Christina Newkirk
Tracy A. Newkirk
Diane I. Newlon
Fred & Joyce Nicholas
Langdon & Dawn Nichols
Mr. & Mrs. Edwin C. Nilan
Mr. & Mrs. Richard E. Nilan
Mr. & Mrs. Ralph C. Noah
Mr. & Mrs. Gerald Noble
Morgan & Cherry Noble
Mr. & Mrs Thomas P. Nock
Jared & Nancy Nodelman
Robert & Harriet Noone
Mr. & Mrs. John B. Norall
Virginia & Robert Norlen
David & Chaney Norman
Patrick & Joanne Norman
Paul & Gloria Norman
Mr. & Mrs. E. John Northwood
John & Carol Northwood
Dolores & Forbes Norris
Dr. & Mrs. Robert W. Noyes
Ron & Hannah Nunn
Elizabeth Nutting Family

O

Victor & Clara Obninsky
Dr. & Mrs. Robert Ockner
Susan & John O'Connell
Douglas & Nadine O'Connor
Alice A. Offill
Dr. & Mrs. Paul C. Ogden
Dick & Ann O'Hanlon
Mr. & Mrs Michael A. O'Hanlon
Corinne & Eugene O'Kelly
Jean Johnston Oller
Marilyn A. Olson
Tom & Peggy O'Neill
Frank & Yolande O'Rourke
Dean & Nicole Osbon
Mary T. & Floyd H. Osborn
Mr. & Mrs. Stephen M. Osborn
Charles & Cecelia Osborne
Mr. & Mrs. John Ostrom
Mr. & Mrs. Eldon Ottenheimer
Mr. & Mrs. Richard C. Otter
Mr. & Mrs. Lee Otterson
Clara S. Owen
Justine Oyster

P

John A. Pagani
Phil & Virginia Page
Pan-Pacific Properties
Ann & Jim Paras
Helen Van Cleave Park
Harold & Gertie Parker
Mr. & Mrs. Joseph Russell Parker
Mr. & Mrs. Stephen Parodi
Georg Wesley Parrish
Juliette Parson
Margolo Parson
Sarah & Rebecca Parsons
Mrs. C. W. Partridge
Mary Lou Pasquel
Nancy King Pastoriza
Donald Patten
Mr. & Mrs. James Patten

Mr. & Mrs. Douglas G. Paul
Sandy Keppel Paul
Bob Paulist
Lynn & Dick Payne
Sunshine & Charles Payne
Jeffrey H. Pearce
Mark A. Pearce
Mr. & Mrs. Melville E. Pearce
Richard S. Pearce
Lucille S. Pearson
Michael Pechner
Brian & Thai Peck
Leonard & Charlotte Peck
Mr. & Mrs. Eric Pedley
Frank & Elizabeth Peebles
Dr. & Mrs. C. J. Peetz, Sr.
Kenneth Robert Peifer
John & Carolyn Pelkan
Harold Pepperell
Anthony Perles
Mr. & Mrs. Fred Perry
Damon & Gloria Peterson
Henry W. Peterson
Martie Jean Peterson
Mary Atterbury Peterson
Ralph & Helen Petersen
Walter & Adrienne Petraitis
Mary E. Petricka
A. Preston Petty
Mr. & Mrs. J. Michael Phelps
Ralph & Helen Phillips
Donald S. Pickett
Mr. & Mrs. Edward F. Pilgram
Mr. & Mrs. Douglas M. Pirie
Gerald & Sandra Pisani
Tim & Laura Pisani
Margot Plant
Joseph Pope
Alison Powell
Beth Anne Powell
Pamela Powell
Drs. Malcolm & Andrea Powell
Joyce Power
Flora & Michael Praszker
Eunice S. Pratt
Robert Edwin Praun
William Bradford Praun
Mr. & Mrs. Ed Price
Mrs. Lee B. Price
Steve Price
Tom & Jeanne Price
Mr. & Mrs. George F. D. Pridmore
Rebecca Winslow Pringle
Robert Bernard Pringle
Martha & Tom Procter
Mr. C. Michael Pruett
Mr. & Mrs. Charles W. Pruett
Daniel Jerome Pruett
Mr. & Mrs. Stephen Pruett-Jones
Robin & Nancy Pryor
Evan & Barbara Pugh
Edwin & Nancy Purdy
Mrs. Charles Purnell
Marcia & Gene Purpus
Inez Mary Purser

Q

Manuel & Mafalda Quartin-Bastos
Bruce D. Quinn
Mr. & Mrs. David H. Quinn, Jr.
Gene Quinn

R

Mr. Damon Raike

Mr. & Mrs. John E. Ratliff
Eloise & Gene Rauscher
Arno Rayner
Martha Reed Read
William & Rosetta Reagles
Edgar & Eileen Reed
James F. Reed
Reed School
Reed School Parent-Teacher Club
Reed Union School District
Robert & Patricia Reeves
Ed & Stephanie Regan
Joe Regelski
Neil & Trudy Reid
Kevin Reilly
Thomas F. Reilly M.D.
Kathy Reiman
Jack Reisner
Tutt & John Remak
Lauren Anne Renna
Jeffrey H. Reusche
Heidi & Christian Reuter
Mr. & Mrs. Kenneth R. Reuter
Jane Ann Rey
Clarke & Marjorie Reynolds
Mr. Terry Melvin Reynolds
Sybil & James Reynolds
Shoshana Bonnie Reznek
Bede & E. Russell Rice III
Denis T. Rice
Edward Russell Rice IV
Mary & Edward Rice
Michael W. Rice
Timothy Wilmans Rice
Daniel G. Richardi
Jeannette & Lawrence Richards
Richardson Bay Audubon Center
Arthur & Jane Richardson
Charles M. Richardson, Jr.
Philip & Grace Richardson
Mr. & Mrs. Howard L. Richcreek
Mr. & Mrs. Douglas Richter
Evon & Stephen Rieden
Jerry & Suzanne Riessen
Jane G. Ring
Mr. & Mrs. Jack Rising
Michelle & Dusty Roads
Gaylord E. Robb
William V. Roberson
Colleen & David Roberts
Dexter & Brenda Roberts
Don & Anne Robinson
Gordon & Adina Robinson
Dr. & Mrs. Harold H. Robinson
Ken & Marsha Roby
William & Wanda Roby
Dennis & Carol Ann Rockey
Acacia M. Rodriguez
Rafael & Acasia Rodriguez
Hans Roenau
Camden & Mary Rogers
Mr. & Mrs. Robert E. Rogers
Barbara Rogers-Levy
Maureen & Rick Roland
Mr. & Mrs. Michael Romer
Mel & Ruth Ronick
Ellen Rony
Mr. & Mrs. Donald Root
Mr. & Mrs. Fred M. Rose
Rick & Kathy Rose
Daniel M. Rosen, M.D.
Bruce & Sylvia Ross
Bruce Ross Family
David Duncan Ross
Dr. & Mrs. Frank Rossman

Edgar J. & Patricia J. Rothenberg
Mr. & Mrs. Samuel Rothstein
Dr. & Mrs. Jirayr Roubinian
Mr. & Mrs. Jack Barton Roxton
Ruth & Richard Rozen
Shirley & Arthur Rude Jr.
Rumsey Family
Dr. Gary W. & Patricia R. Runes
Carol & Wally Rush
Grace & Edward Russell
Edward & Barbara Ryall

S

Juanita Sacks
Gregory B. Saffell
Mr. & Mrs. John A. Sage
Peter A. Salz
Terry Samilson
Dr. & Mrs. Bruce J. Sams, Jr.
Robert H. San-Chez, Jr.
Mr. & Mrs. Avtar Singh Sandhu
Francis & Margaret Sanborn
Mrs. Joseph Sanfilippo
Eric D. Sanford
John E. Sanford
Sarah H. Sanford
Walter E. Sanford
Phyllis & Lewis Sarasy
Sausalito Historical Society
Save Our Libraries Committee
Willard & Frances Saville
Mr. & Mrs. George Sayre
Robert & Cherril Scarth
Edie & John Schaller
Mr. & Mrs. Adrian E. Scharlach
Carmen M. Schleiger
Eric A. Schleiger
Capt. & Jane Schellenberg
Mike & Barbara Schilling
Leslie Schlesinger
Laura Levers Schley
Bill & Liddy Schmidt
Hal & Liz Schmidt
Russ & Bernice Schneider
Russell & Diana Schneider
David & Julie Schoenstadt
Randi & Stacey Schoenstadt
Marcelle Scholl
Mr. & Mrs. Robert B. Schoonmaker
Theodore & Barbara Schrock
Steven & Sally Schroeder
Catherine & Jerry Schuepbach
Duane R. Schukar
Mr. & Mrs. Donald R. Schumacher
Mary Schwartz & Family
Ben & Yvonne Schwarz
Mr. & Mrs. J. Schwendig
Mrs. Ann Y. Scoma
Mrs. Wallace Scott
Steve & Marian Sears
Eric Seelenfreund
Emma Jane & Tyler W. Seeley
Mr. & Mrs. Richard J. Selmeier
Jim & Kay Semrau
Select Business Investments, Inc.
Angelo & Kathryn Servino
Mr. & Mrs. Manu Shamsavari
John & Emily Shaw
Brian & Holly Sheehan
Greg & Sheila Sheehan
Robert & Jane Sheeks
Ralph & Jan Sheets
Carole & Douglas Sheft
Anne Shellabarger

Donna J. Haynie Shepherd
Mr. & Mrs. Walter M. Shields
Mr. & Mrs. Alan F. Shirek
Robert & Dianne Sickler
Colleen & John Silcox
Frank & Jamie Silva
Janet & "Scruffy" Silva
Mr. & Mrs. Donald A. Simon
Ronald & Margaret Simpson
Whit Simpson
Dale Adams Sims
Richard M. Sims, Jr.
M. & V. Silveria
Mr. Carter D. Siverson
Robert Skutch
Regina & Karl Slacik
Frances & Betsy Slavich
Edgar M. Sliney
Ethel Margaret Slocum
Richard & Jean Slottow
John H. Smissaert
Carter B. Smith
Craig Emerson Smith
Consuelo & Alaister Smith
Diane & Larry Smith
Mr. & Mrs. Glen H. Smith
Hap & Z. Smith
Henry B. Dunlap Smith
John J. & Margaret Smith
Dr. & Mrs. P. Dunlap Smith
Dr. & Mrs. Roger H. Smith
Sydney & Janie Smith
Mr. Todd M. Smith
Mr. & Mrs. Warren C. Smith
William & Jodie Smith
William A. & Sandra M. Smith
Peter & Sara Snoek
Mr. & Mrs. Edward Soares
Dr. & Mrs. Yung Jai Sohn
Jo Anne Solberg
Mary E. & Louie Soldavini
Robert & Renee Soleway
Robert & Helen Solinger
Mrs. Oliver Sollom
Capt. Kenneth J. Sommers
Sandra Lyn Sommers
Lucille D. Spangler
Norman & Sally Spencer
Richard & Kay Spencer
Louis & Bonnie Spiesberger
Richard & Joanne Spotswood
Mr. & Mrs. Milton L. Stannard, Jr.
Richard & Joyce Stansbury
George Staubli
Mr. & Mrs. John M. Steadman
Mr. & Mrs. Roderick M. Steele
Mr. & Mrs. Gerhard Stefandl
Holly Stein
Jeffrey & Peyton Stein
Taylor & Todd Stein
Allan Steinau
Marilyn Steinau
Stefan Steinbach
Bart & Brad Stephens
Mr. & Mrs. Edward J. Stephens
Dr. & Mrs. Stuart Stephens
Patricia Stevens
William Allen Stevens
Jason Stewart
Scott Stewart
Mr. & Mrs. Hiram Stickney
Edward & Janice Still
Charles E. Stine
Anna Conley Stock

Mr. & Mrs. Bert Stocking
Joanne Stokes
Marilyn P. Stolte
Theodore A. Stolte
David & Vicki Stollmeyer
Harry & Georgianna Stone
Robert J. Stone
Lawrence & Ruth Stotter
Mrs. Carol J. Stranzl
Carol & Larry Strasburger
Gorden Weld Strawbridge
Roger C. Strawbridge
Elizabeth Stromberg-Baker
Bill & Tracy Strong
Mr. & Mrs. A. K. Strotz
Adam & Katherine Strunk
Dr. George Sugarman
Frank E. & Joyce Sullivan
Mrs. Frederic Supple, Sr.
Willetta & Irvin Sutley
Robert & Sandra Swanson
Sweden House Bakery
John T. & Mary D. Sweeney
Robin R. Sweeny
Mr. & Mrs. William R. Sweet
Joe & Mary Symons

T

Dr. & Mrs. Lewis J. Taich
Jeffrey M. Taich
Jennifer S. Taich
Bert Talbot
Jerry & Elizabeth Talbot
Dr. & Mrs. Leo Tarantino
Judi P. Tawney
Joyce & Donald Tayer
Benjamin R. Taylor
Charles & Jean Taylor
Flora & James L. Taylor
Fred & Kathleen Taylor
Margaret Taylor
Thomas Swift Taylor
Mr. & Mrs. W. Peck Taylor
David & Louise Teather
Jeff & Christine Teather
Mr. Larry Telford
John & Christine Telischak
Jacques & Sandra Terhell
Mary & Bill Terrell
Karin & Rufus Thayer
Mrs. Kathryn Calonge Thomas
Andrew Lang Thompson
Leda Elizabeth Thompson
Mr. Renold Thompson, Jr.
Mrs. Mitzi Thornton
Bill & Barbara Thorsen
Nicholas & Yvonne Thurmond
The Tiburon Land Company
Tiburon Lodge
Tiburon Peninsula Club
Tiburon Yacht Club
Ralph & Eleanor Tierney
Mr. & Mrs. Ray Tilley
Isabel Tinning
Haskell & Janice Titchell
Mr. Jim Titus
Erika & Eric Tjensvold
Norman Todhunter
Chrie J. Tomsick
Frank Tomsick
Peter M. Torrente
Mrs. Wm. E. Towne
Anne B. Tredway
Dick & Dorothy Trezevant

Al & Maurine Trimbach
Mr. & Mrs. James Triplett
Donn K. Trousdale
McLoughlin & Chiquette Trousdale
Ramon & Benita Truman
Catherine Tryon
William Paul Tryon
Rev. Lloyd Tupper
Ann & Marshall Turner
Michael S. Turrini
Carl Twentier
Connee Tyler & Family

U

Kivei Sang & Michele U
Mr. & Mrs. Thomas Uhry
Dr. & Mrs. John A. Ungersma

V

Bob & Lani Valentine
Robert & Jane Van Blaricom
Henry Van Bergen
Robin Ericson Vance
Jeffrey Van Cleve
William van der Ploeg
Crestienne Van Keulen
Michael & Rankin Van Keulen
Alex & Elsie Van Keuren
Barney & Neva Van Ogle
Dr. Theodore & Nancy van Ravenswaay
Enid M. Varney
Arnold E. Vasa
Susan R. Vasa
Dr. & Mrs. Thomas R. Vaughn
Drs. Hans & Ilza Veith
R. W. & Barbara Vickrey
Shirley & Herman Victor
Eugene & Sylvia Vigno
Mr. Bill Vincent
Mr. G. S. Vincent
Roger Vincent
Warren Vincent
Mr. & Mrs. Phillip F. Vizcarra
Lewis & Holly Vogler
Bill von Lackum
Graydon & Jean Voorhies

W

Don Waldbillig
Don & Elspeth Walker
Janet & John Walker
Mr. & Mrs. S. Thompson Walker

William Wallace Jr. Family
Bob & Judy Wallerstein
Virginia M. Walsh
Robert & Lucy Walton
Stephen Wanat
Diane & Kenneth Ward
James A. Wardrop
Helen G. Warren
Watermark Books
Mr. & Mrs. Reed Waters
Peter Waterstreet
Ann & Robert Watson
Dr. & Mrs. George A. Watson
James & Susanne Wattson
Charles B. & Elizabeth L. Waud
Kurt & Sue Webb
Dr. Anna L. Webster
Bruce Cameron Webster
Dr. & Mrs. Robert Webster
Simone & Wayne Wedell
Anna & Will Weinstein
Philip & Elizabeth Weinstein
Dr. & Mrs. Sheridan Weinstein
Carol Weiss
Mrs. Henry J. Weisser
Robert & Mary Welch
Marion Johnston Welish
Theodore & Grace Wellman
Mr. James H. Wells
Mr. & Mrs. Robert S. Wells
Klaus & Ellen Werner
Dorothy Weseth
Jim & Cathy Westberg
Nancy & Robert Westberg
David & Susan Weymouth
Bert & Cheryl Wheeler
Carolyn Wheeler
Kelly Wheeler
Penny J. & Thomas C. White
George & Lucia Whitney
Dr. William W. Whitson
Mr. & Mrs. Malcolm K. Whyte
Leon & Danelle Wiatrak
Robert E. Wickersham
Mr. & Mrs. Donald Wiebe
Corinne Wiley
Doris A. Wilhelm
Mr. & Mrs. Wayne Wilkinson
Edith & Leon Willat
Aaron & Betty Williams
Bill & Pat Williams
Dan & Jan Williams
Mr. & Mrs. Denis Williams
Jamie J. Williams

Jill D. Williams
Laurie & Robb Williams
Virginia E. Williams
John L. Williams
Mr. & Mrs. D. Willoghby
Ryan Stephen Wilsey
Brian & Candy Wilson
Charles B. Wilson
Donald R. Wilson
Joan & Bill Wilson
Joan & Jim Wilson
Mr. & Mrs. Joe R. Wilson
Joyce Wilson
Joyce & Adrian Wilson
Peggy Johnston Wilson
Edith & Leon Willat
Marguerite & Frederick Winn
Mr. & Mrs. Charles J. Winton
Mr. & Mrs. Charles J. Winton III
Doris & Russ Wischow
Mr. & Mrs. W. C. Witter
Everett & Jane Witzel
Dr. & Mrs. Kenneth Woeber
Bruce & Linda Wolfe
Nellie & Harold Wold
Grace McCombie Wolfe
Ed & Kim Wolkenmuth
Mary Helen Wollam
Charles & Virginia Wollborg
John T. Wollman
Annie & Frank Wolverton
Gloria & Bill Wong
Gerald A. Wood
Richard & Christine Wood
Trent Wood
Mrs. Thomas D. Woodward
Mr. & Mrs. James R. Worms
Mrs. Edwin Jack Wylie

Y

Lee A. Yeager
Frank & Betty Yorkis
Julia & Floyd Yost
Ben & Millie Young
Mr. & Mrs. R. A. Young
Mr. R. A. Young III
Ruth D. & John C. Young

Z

Mr. & Mrs. Edward Zelinsky
Mrs. Fred Zelinsky
Ed & Marie Zeller
Dr. & Mrs. Calvin Zippin

The Landmarks Society deeply appreciates the support of the sponsors listed above. Every effort was made to insure that the names of sponsors were correct. For any error which has managed to survive we offer our sincere apology.

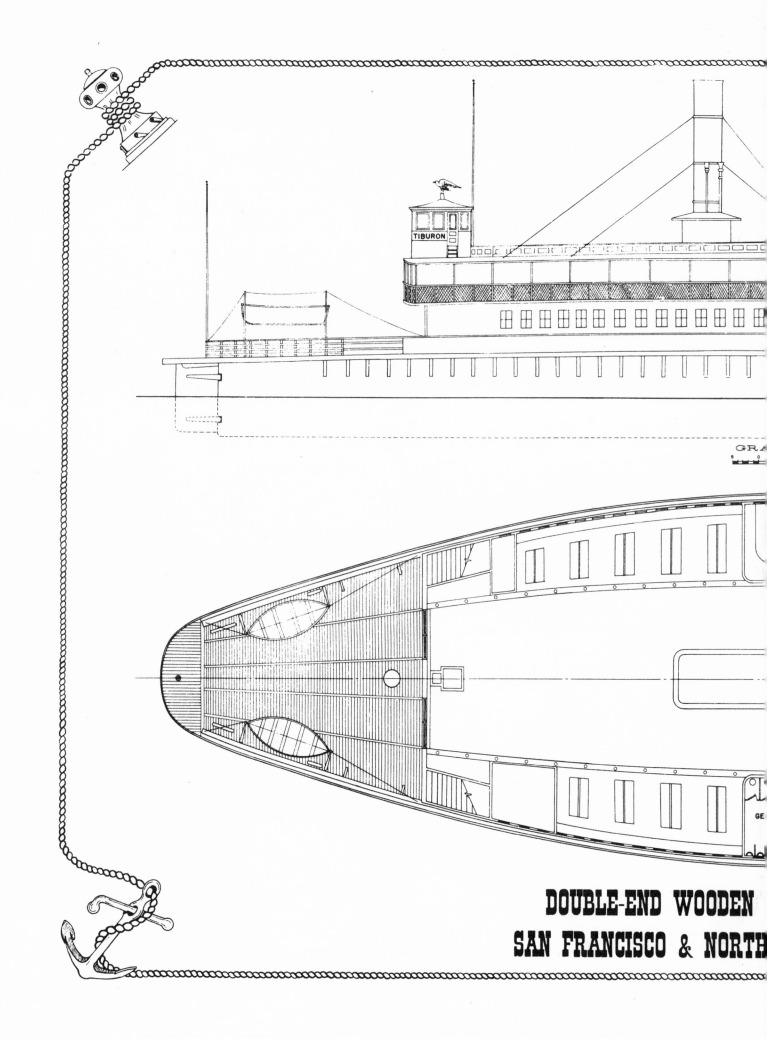

TIBURON

GRA

DOUBLE-END WOODEN

SAN FRANCISCO & NORTH